FOREWORD BY WARREN MOON

When I retired from football, after playing six years in the Canadian Football League and seventeen years in the National Football League, I went to work for my agent, Leigh Steinberg. I was head of business development when Leigh hired Dave as his COO, which morphed into his CEO. I was struck immediately by Dave's energy, his good aggressiveness, his organizational skills, and his engaging personality. The more I worked with him, the more I admired his business acumen and intelligence as well as his demeanor. In little time, Dave was actually at the helm of the company. Dave systematically tackled each hurdle enabling the firm to prosper. No matter how potentially stressful a situation would be, Dave never flinched or showed frustration. He simply worked that much harder all the while maintaining a positive attitude.

Dave and I hit it off right away. We both loved sports and had played football, and, perhaps, I would have met him earlier – on the gridiron – had I and my Washington Huskies faced him and his Occidental College Tigers in the Rose Bowl instead of Michigan. Beyond that, I could tell that his philosophy and work ethic meshed well with my beliefs on what lead to success, both in business and in life. As time progressed, I felt that if the opportunity presented itself, Dave and I would make good business partners; and, finally, it did.

I called Dave to see what he thought about us working together, and he indicated that it was a great idea. Sports 1 Marketing evolved from our subsequent discussions, and we were pleased how quickly things took off. Among other things, Dave brought with him his love to educate and immediately established a training program similar to the one he had at Leigh's office. He is a great communicator. I think a number of young interns come into our office intimidated by, perhaps, me and, perhaps, business in general. But inevitably, Dave's personality enables them to relax. He gets them to listen and has their respect early. They start to adopt his business and life philosophies. He has them on calls and involved in deals almost immediately so that they have a hands-on view of how business works. And he arranges for them to attend some fun and very exciting events. They all go on to have valuable and productive experiences. I have received many letters from interns who have worked at Sports 1 Marketing describing how their lives were changed as a result of their internships and how much it would help them going forward with their careers.

It's great to be able to do something you love and, as huge sports fans, we feel our business keeps us involved in something we are passionate about. And I think I've provided a good balance for Dave. I've been able to get him to slow down on occasion and see the bigger picture – something I am good at – and then his drive, enthusiasm, and determination take things to the next level. This is how we work well together, along with a willingness to communicate immediately if we have our differences. But Dave and I are not only business partners, we are also close friends. In fact, don't be surprised at Halloween to see us dressed as the Arnold Schwarzenegger and Danny DeVito characters from the film *Twins*.

It's been a great ride to date, Dave, and we're just getting started. Good luck with this book.

Warren Moon:
Canadian Football Hall of Fame Inductee 2001
Professional Football Hall of Fame Inductee 2006

CONNECTED
to GOODNESS

Manifest Everything You Desire in Business and Life

DAVID MELTZER

CONTENTS

DEDICATION

I dedicate this book and my journey to my beautiful wife, Julie, and our four amazing children – my M & Ms – Marissa, Mia, Marlena, and Miles. May you and all who you attract stay connected to goodness!

PREFACE

Besides my business partner, Hall of Fame Quarterback Warren Moon, one of my other all-time favorite football players was quarterback Jim McMahon. Enjoying an illustrious fourteen year career in the NFL, McMahon was one of the toughest, hard-working players I've ever had the extreme good fortune to watch. Although he played with a few teams during his tenure, his stint with the Chicago Bears was the most memorable, and one particular game in 1985, the year the Bears won the Super Bowl, I believe best exemplifies his character.

McMahon was suffering from a back injury that required a two-night hospital stay and traction, and he'd missed practice the week leading up to their game against the Vikings. On game day, Bears Coach Mike Ditka took one look at his QB, who also had a leg infection, and said, "You're not playing."

McMahon smirked, "There's no possibility I'm not playing."

Ditka kept McMahon on the bench for three quarters, and the Bears, well, sucked. Finally, after relentless badgering by McMahon, Ditka put him in – and the team, as one, immediately came alive. On his first play in, McMahon called an audible and launched a bullet to Willie Gault. One play, 70 yards, touchdown. The Bears then got possession on a fumble. McMahon called another audible, and this time hit Dennis McKinnon in the end zone. Two plays, two touchdowns. The Bears wiped the field with the Vikings after that.

Not only does this show McMahon's ability to overcome adversity, but it's also an excellent analogy of how one person can inspire a host of others to peak performance or to thrive. By being your best, you are transformed, and you automatically transform others around you.

I, myself, experienced a major transformation, and I am here to transform you. At the time of my life when I looked to have it all, I was actually lost and quickly heading in the wrong direction. My downward spiral, however, turned out to be a necessary journey. Along the way, I found the recipe for success that allowed me to reinvent myself, find true peace and happiness, and inspire others. My goal now is to save you the time and money I spent and lost – and make your journey easier than mine.

From someone who has gone from rags to riches, back to rags, then back to riches, I promise you that my formula for achievement works – my seven Principles, each with its own four Key Elements. You will enjoy fulfillment and prosperity, and be able to manifest what you desire more accurately and rapidly. But most importantly, you will be happy and feel good. In fact, if you follow my seven interrelated Principles, not only will you attain success beyond your wildest imagination, but you'll be able to go one step further and help others to thrive. Individuals like Robert Kraft, owner of the New England Patriots, Paul Allen of Microsoft, and former NFL quarterback Warren Moon experienced this same transformation; and not only did they thrive, but like the Chicago Bears when Jim McMahon entered the game, others around them thrived too.

Yes, I've been blessed with many brilliant mentors over the years, all of whom have been exceptionally generous with their wisdom. Some of them readily shared their knowledge, while others set an example by their actions, both good and bad. For instance, when I was CEO for sports "Super Agent" Leigh Steinberg (the movie *Jerry Maguire* was based on Leigh), he accelerated my growth by providing me unbelievable advice even though he was struggling with his own transformation. Beyond "do as I say, not as I do," Leigh simply said, "Dave, if you ever are wondering what to do when it comes to business, just remember – never negotiate to the last penny, always be fair, and don't do business with dicks."

But let me also credit the least famous of all my mentors, my grandfather, who planted the seeds with respect to my basic philosophies of what I now strive for in life – to make lots of money, help lots of people, and have lots of fun. This is also my mantra, mission statement and vision that I chant and meditate on. My grandfather had told me that you only require three things in life to be happy: "You need to find one partner who is your liaison between you, your family, and your friends. You need to find one job that you love. And, finally, you need to buy the best bed that you can find." These pearls of wisdom transformed into my business and life objectives. The first pearl about "you and your spouse or partner as the liaison" became, in part, my objective to "help a lot of people". "Make a lot of money" came from being passionate about work. And "having lots of fun", well, that has a lot to do with my grandfather's advice about the "bed".

Every day I now am able to easily manifest my desires, and if you follow my Principles, you will be able to manifest whatever it is you want as well. But, morphing from my grandfather's to my more modern, aligned philosophies did not come by accident or coincidence. Like I've said, I needed to stumble along the way.

We all need to travel on our own journeys. The voyage is where each of us learns, and nothing can be more rewarding than overcoming adversity. But I want you to avoid many of the trips and falls that I experienced. I want you to be like the many athletes and celebrities who I have helped through their own self-actualization and transformation. I want you to be able to enjoy the rewards and satisfaction that emanates from my three basic philosophies. I want you to learn from my seven Principles so that you, too, will become enlightened and manifest whatever it is you want in life and in business. My goal is to get you to thrive, meaning to manifest anything and everything you could ever want in life and in business and to perpetuate that manifestation for yourself and others.

I promise you, the universe is abundant. There is enough of everything for everybody.

Get ready for an immense and exciting transformation in how you do business and live your life.

Get ready to thrive!

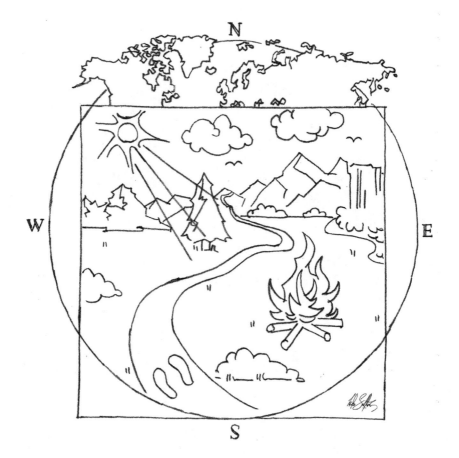

HOW IT ALL BEGAN

I know why I was born. Anyone who can say that is blessed.

I'll start my story in law school. I went to Tulane. This marked the first decision I ever made strictly for myself. Up to this point, my family and the expectations of others drove all of my other decisions. I had visited the school and, quite simply, I fell in love with it. Among other things on my visit, I met John Kramer, Dean of Tulane University Law School and he promised me, "If you come to Tulane, I'll personally take care of you."

My first encounter with Dean Kramer took place in the lobby of the law school. He sensed I was lost and asked me if I needed any help. A brief conversation ensued, and I explained to him that I was deciding between Tulane and two other prestigious schools. At that point, he actually invited me out to lunch.

I guess my natural sales abilities came to the forefront. We ended up getting along tremendously. Of course, a couple of buckets of beer and two entrees, which I soon learned he had ordered just for himself, certainly helped, but this was New Orleans after all. Anyway, I felt that this relationship alone would be more valuable than anything any of the other prestigious law schools, which had also accepted me, could offer.

So, here I was, everything going along smoothly just as my family and friends had always promised – until in my second year of law school when my oldest stepbrother, a doctor, called and told me he had HIV. Having fulfilled his lifelong dream of becoming a doctor, he'd always told me growing up, "Make sure you're not just well-trained, but that you're also well-educated." He also said, "Do what *you* want to do, not just what others want you to do."

And now, he was dying. This had a great effect on me as, up to this point, most things in life had gone my way. At roughly this same time, I also lost my pending summer clerkship, a well-paying job, because of the economy and a lack of funding. How was I going to pay back all of the loans I had taken out for law school, or get additional loans? I had no job and I had no credit; my stepfather had used and then failed to pay back my credit cards in trying to start a new business, effectively ruining my credit. Tulane was now threatening to kick me out, and even my buddy, the dean, who tried to look for grant money, scholarships and jobs for me, had no control over Equifax and my destroyed credit. On top of this, the stress of my stepbrother's illness and subsequent death put too much of a strain on the marriage between my mother and stepfather, and they divorced.

In a matter of two weeks, everything that I had dreamed about and worked so hard for were gone. When I came home for my stepbrother's funeral, I broke the news to my mother.

"Mom, I've received a job offer to sell golf clubs in Japan. It pays $60,000 plus commissions."

"You're not quitting law school," she replied firmly.

One of my uncles chimed in. "If you don't invest in yourself, what are you ever going to invest in?"

This really struck a chord with me. This same uncle offered to pay for the rest of my law school education. Not wanting to feel beholden to him or the pressure that I felt came with the money, I declined; but we did reach an agreement whereby he co-signed on my law loans and told me that he'd help me if I couldn't make a payment. So, I invested in myself and returned to Tulane – thank the universe!

I had a fantastic time my third year in law school. I had the opportunity to work for the law school's civil clinic. Under a supervising attorney's guidance, I was sanctioned by the Louisiana Bar to practice, even though I was only a third year law student; and I won a jury trial in 5th Circuit Federal Court on the grounds of cruel and unusual punishment on behalf of an inmate who had been abused by a prison guard. At that time, it was the largest judgment ever awarded in a case brought by a Tulane student.

This lead to a flood of job offers. One in particular came by way of a law professor friend, A.N. Yiannopoulos, who I had traveled to Greece with the summer after my first year in law school as part of Tulane's Admiralty Program abroad. Greece was another early example of me learning to stand up for myself over the objections of others. In this instance, the opposition came from my family, who felt that I should not be borrowing more money at that time. To the contrary, I thought, "What's an extra $2,500 for an opportunity to study in Greece when I'm already $100,000 in debt?"

Professor Yiannopoulos had been hired years before by West Publishing, the world's largest legal publisher, to explain and analyze the Napoleonic Code, which was really the first influential and far-reaching set of modern laws. Professor Yiannopoulos had become West Publishing's highest paid author as his civil treaties sold extremely well worldwide. Through his relationship with West Publishing, he knew of an employment opportunity at one of the newest divisions, Westlaw. The year was 1993, the job involved the then new field of the Internet, and his influence at West Publishing secured me an interview.

Among other things, West Publishing was and still is the official reporter of case law and statutes for all fifty states and the federal government. West's digesting system, which breaks the law down into numbered topics and subcategories of issues, had worked for over a hundred years in book form, and transitioned beautifully to computer with the advent of the CD-ROM. The Westlaw division of

West Publishing was the next step. Westlaw was going to put legal research online.

There were 2,500 applicants for the four initial sales positions at Westlaw, and neither I nor most anyone else in the world had any idea what "online" meant at that time. In the early 1990s, the entirety of the Internet consisted of .edu, Lexis-Nexis, and Westlaw. So, not only did I not know what the Internet was, but having grown up in San Diego, attending college in Los Angeles and law school in New Orleans, I was clueless about freezing cold winters when I went for my final interviews at the company's headquarters in Minnesota. I didn't even own an overcoat, so I had to borrow one for the trip.

I was anxiously waiting in the lobby at the Marriott Residence Inn in Eagan, Minnesota when the car arrived to pick me up for my interview. Draped over the chair next to me was an overcoat. As I put it on, a guy immediately started yelling at me, "Hey, you've got my coat! You've got my coat!" In the midst of my denial, I realized that, due to my nervousness, I had put his overcoat on over the borrowed coat I was already wearing.

I didn't help my already frazzled nerves when, on the way to the interview, the car hit an ice patch, then slid off the road and crashed. I'm sure it was only a coincidence that the accident occurred after I told the driver, a die-hard Minnesota Vikings' fan, that my team was the San Diego Chargers.

It was only a minor fender bender, but now, completely discombobulated, I arrived at West Publishing. On the way to the first of six final interviews, as I anxiously rode the elevator to the Executive Offices on the 6th floor, I shared my short ride with this slightly balding guy. I turned to him and quipped, "Grass doesn't grow on a busy street." The gentleman then introduced himself as Vance Opperman, son of West Publishing's CEO, Dwight Opperman. Fortunately for me as I was not wearing Depends at the time, Vance had laughed. Later, when Vance became CEO, he said to me over drinks, "That was the best line I've ever heard about going bald."

I went through my first round of interviews being the youngest lawyer by at least ten years. So, I am now in for my last interview with Lou Lombardi, a vice president, who had worked his way up from the stockroom, while the other guys at West were all lawyers. Lou ran the sales force and was so important to West that they let him keep his office in Westbury, New York rather than insisting he relocate to Minnesota. This also kept Lou, a New York Jets fan, safe from the same car service driver I'd had.

Toward the end of my interview, Lou said, "You don't have the experience that everyone else has. Why should I hire you?"

Using a strategy that I call "Penn Value" (which I will discuss later in the book), I replied, "Look, you can pay me the salary plus expenses but keep my commissions if I am not in the top half of all of the sales guys – and you can then fire me. You have nothing to lose."

Of course, I knew that the salary and expenses alone regardless of commissions were going to be more than what I would have made as, say, a District Attorney in New Jersey. Therefore, I knew that I had nothing to lose.

At that point, Lou looked at me and asked, "Do you have a girlfriend?"

Not knowing where Lou was going with this question, I cautiously replied, "Yes."

"Do you have a picture of her?"

I withdrew a little photo from my wallet (remember, those days were prior to cell phones) and handed it to him.

Lou studied it for a moment or two before snorting, "If an ugly guy like you can sell yourself to a girl like this, you can definitely sell my stuff."

For those who know me, I, for once, was speechless and had no idea what Lou was thinking until he then broke into a wide grin, which effectively said, "You're hired."

Lou became one of my first mentors for sales as well as for life. He and I became and will remain close friends forever. I am deeply grateful for Lou and other great mentors that I was able to attract along my journey

Once again, I had resisted the trend of listening to others – who said that I wouldn't be a real lawyer if I took this job. Family and friends thought I was insane selling this thing called "the Internet". But I enjoyed sales and quickly discovered I had a knack for it. I have just always been one of those people who could sell "pork products to orthodox rabbis". I just didn't realize when I was young that I could make a profession out of it. From early on, I had been called "an eagle", a natural born salesman (as compared to a "journeyman", someone who has to learn how to sell, and works hard every day to get better).

The summer I lost my internship in law school, I volunteered at a law firm and worked part-time at "Road Runner Sports", where catalogue purchases, at that time, were made over the phone. From 4 a.m. until 9 a.m. (a "beat even the early bird to the worm" drive I maintain to this day, in terms of my mentality, and not for the actual taste of a worm), I would take incoming calls, and I became their number one sales representative. I learned to upsell, which is convincing someone to buy two or more of an item, or something more expensive than they initially intended. Because my shift was 7 a.m. to noon on the East Coast, I also learned how to sell "East Coast style", which is a more forceful and aggressive selling method. I actually woke up at 3:00 a.m. excited to go to Road Runner Sports and dreaded going to the legal research job later in the afternoon.

In any event, I was one of four who made up Westlaw's initial sales force. Our job was to sell their combo – a CD, which you could search the same way you looked for information online, and the actual online product. Remember, at that time, people did not know about the Internet. Not everyone had modems, and you could search a CD more rapidly. Westlaw, however, eventually transitioned completely over to the Internet and phased out the CD.

West was so big, wealthy, powerful and structured, they provided tremendous training, both initially and on an ongoing basis. I received training in everything from law to sales to business to antitrust. Because the Internet and Internet business was in a state of "pre-chasm", West was a unique employer. They had access to data and the money for training that most other companies did not; "pre-chasm" is when only the early adopters know of and use a product, while "chasm" is when a product is accepted and used by the masses.

Once Westlaw went online, it became a huge differentiator with major advantages in the marketplace. You could now search and find everything you needed online, proving wrong all of the skeptics, from Supreme Court Justices on down, who said that the books would never be replaced. In fact, Westlaw grew so quickly that I started doing the trainings within my first year. This all helped me to become a combination of an eagle and a journeyman. Think of this in athletic terms. Michael Jordan and Tiger Woods are naturally gifted, but it is their discipline and hard work that made them more successful than others.

After six months, Westlaw had to change the compensation plan with respect to me because I was making far too much money. Within nine months, I had outsold the other salespeople three to one. Within this time frame, I had paid off all of my law school loans, and bought my mother a house and a car. I pinched myself every day. I thought this was luck. So long as I was out of debt and had provided for my mom, at least I could say that I'd been a success for a while, and I had not let my mom down if and when reality returned.

At Westlaw, I continued to learn new sales techniques, such as "spin selling" and "solution selling"; these are two "features and benefits" type of sales trainings that encompass building business cases, the values and benefits of a product, overcoming objections, utilizing the right point of sale and the like. It was old IBM, a very Big Blue approach, where sales are treated as a fulfillment of a buyer's needs based on the benefits and features of your product. This is why Westlaw only hired lawyers. Part of "solution selling" is that executives sell only to executives. With Westlaw, lawyers would be selling to lawyers, and would, therefore, be able to speak from a position of credibility. West made sure that our business cards indicated that we were lawyers, thereby giving us a statistically greater chance of success. Lawyers, after all, can speak to other lawyers about, among other things, legal research. We also understood billing and could talk to them about how to bill their clients for the time and cost of online legal research. From a value analysis, Westlaw was thus the first Internet business to figure out how to be a profit center for its subscribers.

I have to say that West treated their sales force like rock stars. This was West's culture. They considered us the top executives in the company. They held nothing back. We received six-figure salaries, as well as reimbursement for expenses, including housing, cars, hotel, travel, food and dry cleaning, and benefits. You were also never going to be fired. You either had to die or retire. What a great first job, especially for someone like me, who grew up financially challenged.

I was the number one sales person for my first three years. My territory was the Southeast, but because of my success, they also put me on specialized campaigns in an attempt to increase their revenue and market share. What I didn't know at the time was that, behind the scenes, West was trying to build value for a potential company sale. During my third year, in 1996, The Thomson Company acquired West Publishing for 3.5 billion dollars. Thomson no longer required that everyone at Westlaw be lawyers. Thompson proceeded to continuously split and cut territories. I was still at the top, but I started venturing off in other directions and exploring other opportunities, such as consulting and increasing my real estate investments.

Key at that time was that the Internet had gone from something virtually unknown when I had started to something now in the midst of a boom, and I had been smart enough to have branded myself an Internet guy, not a lawyer. Even though Westlaw was not technically seen as such, it was one of the first successful "Internet" businesses with one of the Internet's first search engines. In terms of revenue, they were the largest on the Internet. West understood the quantifiable monetization of the Internet – charging for search time and the like which lawyers using the service could then bill back to the clients – well before most others. So, I was an executive of a "pre-chasm" Internet company. I understood the business issues of the Internet. I knew how to sell the Internet.

I was with Westlaw for seven years, during which time West had grown to a $17 billion dollar company in gross revenues. I had become the Sales Director and, directly or indirectly, managed 695 sales representatives. It was during my seventh year that I became aware of the Accenture start-up company, Everypath.

Everypath was a wireless proxy server company that transcoded (converted format for an application) the Internet onto mobile devices like WAP (wireless application protocol) phones and the Palm VII, one of the first wireless data-capable information devices. Everypath was in the same place Westlaw had been in years before, except instead of being a "pre-chasm" Internet business, they were a "pre-chasm" wireless business. I understood the vision that whatever I was doing on the computer, I would eventually be able to do with a hand-held device, and these proxy server companies were the intermediate step. I joined Everypath as their Director of Sales.

Along with this $169 million dollar start-up came the perks of the Internet boom. Drinks and food flowed freely. Money was spent like it was going out of style, all for market share. Through us, companies like E-trade and Alaska Airlines became the early stage Internet for your phones. When I started with Everypath, there were twelve employees. Within two years, it grew to over 350 employees with 52 of them managed by me.

But in the back of my mind, even then, I was thinking that there would eventually be no need for this business because consumers would have hand-held computers. Ironically, or, perhaps, it was serendipity, I met the people from Samsung. They had recently manufactured the world's first convergence device, which wedded wireless, applications and hardware. Running Windows CE, it had a real Windows browser, not a WAP browser. It sold for a pricey $1,700, but it was truly a little computer that looked like a matrix phone, and, although a little bulky, you held it in your hand. The stylus employed bluetooth technology, which was also new; but you could put your phone down, walk sixteen feet away, make your phone call and talk wirelessly through the stylus. At the time, this was incredible. No one else had a wireless hand-held device that could be used to perform Internet, personal computer, cellular phone and organizer functions.

Samsung soon thereafter hired me as CEO of their PC-EPhone CyberBank Division (later known as Samsung U.S.A.) to bring their PC-EPhone to the U.S. Yes, for all of you who find yourself addicted to your smart phone, you can blame me. Samsung initially wanted me as Vice President of Sales, then as their COO, but I flew to Korea and said to their board, "The only job I'm interested in is as your CEO." At that time, it was very chic to be young and a tech CEO, especially one with a law degree. I was an Internet guru who worked, networked, and even played golf with guys like Bill Gates, Michael Dell and Sean Parker. I was one of the keynote speakers at COMDEX in Las Vegas (one of the world's largest computer trade shows at that time) as we won "Best of COMDEX" two years in a row. From there, as the foremost expert on convergence devices, I began traveling the world to speak, including keynote speeches at IT Korea and COMDEX in Sydney and Melbourne, Australia. Back home, I appeared on *Good Morning, America.*

Throughout this process, I was making a load of money. Then Congress enacted the Sarbanes-Oxley Act, which set new or enhanced standards for all U.S. public company boards and management. The Sarbanes-Oxley Act required top management to individually certify the accuracy of financial information dealing with the compliance of corporate officers in raising money. This made me very nervous because I was raising money and signing documents; and now I was, potentially, going to be personally liable for any inaccuracies. I was also sensing that the original Samsung phones were too expensive and bulky and weren't going to be as widely accepted in the U.S. as first thought. On top of that, feeling a sense of responsibility, I had hired a lot of my friends to work for me and gave them jobs that they were incapable of doing. I ended up taking the heat for their inadequacies and poor performance. Given all of the above and my financial position, I thought that this was a good time to semi-retire and become an entrepreneur.

I left on very good terms – the PC-EPhone CyberBank Division now had more than 200 employees with "pre-chasm" revenues of $5 million dollars – and, at the age of thirty-five, I truly became a venture capitalist. I started my own businesses, such as a real estate development and construction company, raised money for other businesses and invested in, among other things, commercial and residential real estate and land. I also wanted to consult in technology, but not "be" in technology; I didn't want all of those people who I worked for to think I'd just used them as a springboard. In retrospect, and as part of my business Principles discussed in Section 2, it was a mistake being so worried about what people would think. I also erred in believing that you're doing an unqualified individual a favor by hiring them. Foolishly, even after my experience at Samsung, I kept allowing this lesson to kick me in the face.

In any event, I continued to invest in real estate; something I had started while at West, where I had formulated a retirement plan. Every year, I would determine where the hottest rental properties were located. I'd do this by finding a rental broker and learning where there were no rentals left for the summer. I'd then buy a property, even if it needed to be rehabbed, at that location. I knew that with rental income, I'd at least break even. I would take out a thirty-year mortgage on each property purchased and effectively get my mortgages down to fifteen years by making bi-monthly payments and double paying at least one installment. This way, by Year Sixteen, I'd own the Year One purchased property outright. Because these properties were in hot rental markets and, historically, property values double every fifteen years, not only would I have doubled my money on some of these properties, but I could then refinance the remainders, bank the tax-free money, and, at a minimum, break even from the others' rental income.

With my system in place, I figured I could retire in Year Sixteen at the age of forty. I would have at least $300,000 of tax-free income coming in per year, which translates into a $500,000 taxable salary. This was all without me ever having to sell a property, and the only thing that I had to do was manage fifteen properties. I followed through with my plan for a few years until the market went crazy. I completely abandoned my system and bought a host of new properties. Could you blame me if I could buy a property for $167,000 and sell it for $850,000? I am still confident that my system was sound and would have worked. But then I would not have gone on my journey and discovered that there was a lot more to life than financial value.

Regardless, here I was semi-retired and an entrepreneur. Some of my investments turned out to be huge mistakes for many reasons.

I had done so well at such a young age that I had friends and family wanting to be a part of my investments; and it didn't matter that some of these investments were extremely risky. For example, I started a corporate connection business where I matched mid-market and Fortune 500 companies with CEOs who could fulfill what had been identified as these company's critical business issues (picture a huge corporate dating service). I also invested in one of the first video streaming companies. Despite my efforts to explain the risk and dissuade others from investing in my ventures, there were negative feelings and guilt when I lost some of my friends' and family's money.

During this time, I had built my wife, Julie, her dream house in Rancho Santa Fe. Let me go on a tangent a moment and tell you a little about my wife. I met Julie in the fourth grade. She was the cousin of one of my close friends, David Jaffe, and she lived one street away from me. She was beautiful then and she continues to grow more beautiful each day. When I saw her for the first time, I fell instantly in love with her, well, on a fourth grade level. But I needed to mature, so it wasn't until I was in sixth grade school camp (a special overnight camp for all 6th graders in San Diego County held during the school year) that I asked her to go steady with me. Apparently, having Rob Blake, my best friend, scream, "Dave wants to go steady with you!" down to the girls' cabins wasn't the maturity level needed to garner love in return, as Julie shouted back, "Tell him 'No', and you tell him to ask me himself!" After returning from camp and totally embarrassed, I did what every other mature twelve-year-old does – I hid in the bushes and threw an egg at her. In the seventh grade, I was Bar Mitzvahed, and thus, officially a man (at least in the eyes of Jewish law, but just try getting a California driver's license). Now that I was a he-man, I designed other, more sophisticated ways to show my affection for Julie – I threw rocks at her – a tradition that continued into the eighth grade. That's when I got word from David Jaffe that, for some inexplicable reason, Julie didn't like me, was afraid of me, and that I should stay away from her.

As time moved on, I would occasionally bump into Julie (and no, despite what you've just read, I don't mean in in a purposeful, physical way meant to inflict injury). In fact, Julie relayed a story later of a conversation that she'd had with her mother. Sadly, this was the last conversation she would have with her mother who was lying in bed and dying of cancer. She told her mother, "I ran into David Meltzer at a bar on his break from law school." Through her pain and moments of confusion caused by her meds, Julie's mother quite coherently replied, "Isn't that the little shit who threw an egg at you?"

Julie updated her on what I was up to, including law school. Upon conclusion, her mom said, "You should date him then."

Julie responded, "He's already dating someone."

After a moment of consideration, her mom said, "Then you should date a guy like him."

Three years later, I was at a crowded bar down in Mexico, on my way to the bathroom, and who should I (literally this time) bump into but Julie? She looked more beautiful than ever. We started talking with me, basically, apologizing for all of my past juvenile behavior. Unfortunately, I was with one of my Westlaw employees, who was quite intoxicated, loud and obnoxious. So despite Julie giving me her number, I was too embarrassed to call her. Imagine my shock and excitement when three weeks later, Julie called me! (I later kidded her that she must have been very desperate). I almost blew it once more on our official first date – a beach day followed by dinner. The first thing out of my mouth when I saw her and the little bag she was holding was, "Oh, I didn't know you were spending the night." Of course, the bag simply contained a change of clothes for dinner.

Back to where I branched off: Julie and I were married, had three children, and at the age of thirty-five, here we were in Rancho Santa Fe. It now shouldn't come as any surprise that I would build the love of my life, whose heart I had somehow won over with my caveman behavior, routinely corrected in Dear Abby columns, the home she felt we would live and die in. However, the very first night we moved in, lying in bed, I felt empty for the first time in my life. I thought, "Oh shit, I made a big mistake." I had been very happy where we were living and had been resistant to the move (I adhere to the millionaire-next-door philosophy, where *they* can have the big house and expensive car, and I'll take the $300,000 house, the $30,000 car and a diversity of investments). And here I was with this multimillion dollar house, something bigger and more expensive than I would ever have wanted to own. The house had no meaning. The expensive cars and expensive trips no longer had meaning. Starting at that moment, I began to disregard everything that had gotten me to that particular point of life, and a pattern of self-sabotage ensued.

I started hanging around with the wrong people. I traveled around the country with guys who were into drugs, heavy drinking, strip clubs and the like. These guys weren't living what I now consider a purposeful existence. In my mind, I wasn't part of that world, despite the fact that I wasn't paying attention to what was really important to me. The whole time I thought myself above these guys, that I'd partake every once in a while, but that it wasn't my lifestyle, and it wasn't having an effect on me. Of course, I was fooling myself. I was working hard, but partying even harder and was oblivious to the cumulative effect of four years.

I remember coming home drunk from the Emmy Awards with rapper Lil Jon at 5 a.m. one morning and Julie waiting for me in our inner courtyard. She looked at me with pure disappointment and said, "You are not a rock star."

I replied, "I may not be, but I sure feel like one."

More upset than I'd ever seen her, Julie said, "Stagger upstairs to one of the guest rooms, and we'll talk when you're sober." And with that, she sent me to a room, away from the family.

In the morning, Julie sat me down, looked me in the eye, and for the first time ever, said, "David, I'm not happy, and you'd better change."

Coincidently, (although there are no coincidences) that same week I went golfing with my old friend, Rob. I asked, "Why haven't I seen you in a while, and why haven't you called?"

He replied, "I don't like who you are becoming, and I definitely don't like the guys you're hanging around with."

"But I'm not like those guys," I pleaded.

Rob looked at me sympathetically and I could hear the truth in his voice as he said, "Dave, you can lie to yourself, but don't lie to me."

These two incidents opened my eyes more quickly than any smelling salts. It was time to return to my authentic self. Unfortunately or, as it turns out fortunately, I now carried with me the cumulative effect of years of not taking accountability for my own actions. It would take me awhile to regenerate the positive energy needed to revive myself.

I became disciplined again. I went back and read Theodore Roosevelt's *The Strenuous Life*, a powerful speech turned book on what is necessary for an overall vital and healthy life. I looked back at the part of my life that had created fulfillment and peace. After much self-reflection, I realized that it had come from waking up every day with a purpose.

One of my investments was Poplar Grove Golf Course in Amherst, Virginia. *Golf Magazine* called it the eighth best new golf course in the country. Owning a golf course had always been a dream of mine and, without knowing it at the time, it was among my first experiences of learning to manifest what I wanted, a concept discussed in Section 2. Within two weeks of my desire to own a golf course, I met the majority owner of Poplar Grove and was offered a 25% interest in the course. Economically, it was the wrong time to buy into a golf course, but it turned out to be the perfect time for me.

When I made this decision, I was not yet aware I was on a spiritual journey, but I felt something almost sacred about Poplar Grove. Indeed, the course turned out to be a very holistic place. It was built on crystals and minerals that only existed in certain areas, similar to Sedona, Arizona with its vortex. Everything at the course was organic.

The majority owner turned out to be an extremely educated, spiritual, and enlightened person. He was my first true spiritual partner. He worked differently, the first person who truly "got out of his own way", a concept that I will be discussing. He told me the story of how Poplar Grove came to be.

"I'd been looking to start a golf course," he began. "And I'd been looking for almost a year, when one night, I drove up here to survey the property. It was pitch black, and I couldn't see a thing. So, naturally, I called my wife."

"To tell her it was too dark?" I chuckled.

"No," he replied. "I called to tell her that I had found my golf course. She asked me what did it look like, and I told her that I didn't know."

But he knew. On a completely different level, he knew. As an aside or, perhaps an addition, it turns out the three tracts of land available for purchase exactly added up to the 2,000 acres he envisioned.

Simultaneous to Poplar Grove, I met and worked with Lee Brower, a multigenerational wealth expert and founder of the internationally recognized educational and philanthropic organization, The Quadrant Living Experience, LLC. Lee was also featured in the book and film, *The Secret*. Lee opened my eyes to the bigger universe out there, my power and my potential. Jack Canfield and Dr. Michael Beckwith from *The Secret* and the spiritual self-help author and motivational speaker Dr. Wayne Dyer also became a part of my life.

Typically, my day began at 4:00 a.m. and ended promptly at 11:00 p.m., but I now found myself up well past my usual bedtime feverously reading anything I could get my hands on. I was starting to understand. As I began to comprehend, I let the universe bring things to me and continued reading books like *The Mastermind* (Napoleon Hill) and *Majesty of Calmness* (William George Jordan).

Through my work with Lee, I now understood manifestation, and I was aware that I could manifest what I wanted when, like Poplar Grove, I created Compliant Company, a "SaaS" (software as a service) solution in the legal realm. It was an area I knew, except it was legal compliance software rather than legal research software. Legal Zoom had been extremely profitable, and I saw a huge market opportunity. Whereas software existed to create business entities, none existed to call, complete or record the meetings, or keep resolutions and the like for these companies. Because of the way Compliant Company worked, I actually invented one of the first online clouds.

While associates ran or managed all of my other investments, I was at the helm of Compliant Company. I was now traveling back and forth from Calcutta, India, where I had 150 developers, and Compliant Company's headquarters in San Diego. During this time, I was still working with Lee, stopping off at Poplar Grove, and reading all that I could. Everything was intertwined. For the first time, I started articulating my beliefs in public. I was now telling people who I was working with, about the spiritual journey I was on, and the different way I was now doing business. I'd say, "Well, 'Corporate Dave' would have done it this way, but me, 'Dave Who Is Starting To Get It', now does it this way, and you need to trust me."

Compliant Company ("CC") was meant to serve a broader purpose in my quest for enlightenment. I think there was a reason that I had started CC in Calcutta, which is a very spiritual place in and of itself. Had I not begun CC, I wouldn't have been traveling to India, and had I not been traveling to India, I would not have been seated next to Dr. Sangeeta Sahi on one particular flight. A complete stranger, she turned and looked at me on that flight and asked, "Are you okay?"

I replied, "I've gone through some tough times, but I'm back on track."

I added cheerfully, "Actually, I'm better than ever."

Dr. Sahi studied me closely, then said, "You carry a lot of energy, but your energy is off. You're blocking your energy and are in your own way."

It blew me away that not only could she read my energy, but she used language identical to what I had heard from Lee and the majority owner of Poplar Grove. At that moment, I realized that I was a neophyte, perhaps a gung-ho neophyte, but still a neophyte who had a lot more to learn.

Dr. Sahi turned out to not only be a medical doctor, but also a holistic accelerator of healing, and a practitioner of Quantum medicine. She offered to work with me. She indicated that she had a workshop where I could learn about Theta meditation and healing.

Let me take one step back. My wife has always been very spiritual. Among other things, Julie had been open to and explored readings, channeling, and past life regressions. I, on the other hand, had always been suspicious, even negative toward this kind of spirituality. I had the stereotype in my mind that these kinds of spiritual individuals were unemployed, broke, undernourished, and always "high" on their mom's couch. I could not understand how these individuals thought they could possibly manifest Publisher's Clearing House coming to their door with a $100 million dollar check.

The workshop turned out to be the first philosophy in learning that I had been exposed to that fit an Albert Einstein/Max Planck/ Spiritual Secret-based physics foundation that I understood and agreed with. I already had as the fundamental basis of my belief system that everything in the universe vibrates – minerals vibrate the slowest, plants vibrate faster, and animals and humans vibrate at the fastest speed. Further, I believed that you can only be aware of those things that vibrate at your speed or less. So, I did not have to make that great of a jump to accept that if I could meditate to increase the vibration of myself, I could be aware of the secrets of the universe, like past life regression and manifestation, that exist at that higher vibrational level. Finally, here was a medical doctor explaining in a scientific way how to utilize my energy by getting out of my own way and letting the flow continue through me.

Dr. Sahi and her workshop served to fill a gap between the spiritual and the physical, and validated my belief in the power of vibration. It provided me with a comfort level. I now understood how I could meditate, create energy and get out of my own way, and it explained what I had perceived as a conflict between trying very hard, yet letting things come to me. Since all but "source energy" (God, Jesus, Buddha or whatever it is you want to call it) have a Ying and a Yang, I grasped how this Ying and this Yang worked together. By the physical nature of vibration and by increasing the vibration of myself, I could raise my awareness and abilities as a result of Theta healing and energy. I realized that I could do all of this with my eyes closed, rather than stoned on my mom's couch, and that I could now truly relate to my wife on a whole different level. I felt so enlightened by what I had learned that I hired Dr. Sahi to do a workshop for CC and friends in San Diego.

So, here I had had this epiphany. I had gone from a feeling of emptiness to feeling fulfilled. Even though I had the effects of bad decisions, bad energy, and people worrying about me, I was in a better space than ever.

As mentioned, CC was the only one of my investments that I was actively running and, after both my wife and my oldest friend had opened my eyes, I felt that I needed another steady job with a purpose. But while I was exploring options, I still had to deal with the negative effects. I had over-extended myself and my finances on the business front. I had people who had acted as my best friends until I could no longer pay or hire them. I had others blaming me for financial losses due to the economy. A neighbor defrauding me for $2.5 million, which I thought had created my financial disaster in the first place, ultimately proved the catalyst for me having to declare bankruptcy.

Compliant Company went under. I lost my interest in Poplar Grove. Julie sat in bed at night worrying about the fact that we could not make the mortgage payments on the house. All the while I, on the other hand, felt at peace knowing that I could manifest whatever it was that I wanted. In fact, I felt so at peace that even my negative thoughts about my corrupt neighbor, which had arisen from me not being accountable for my actions, began to dissipate. I realized that, but for him, I would not be in the holistic place I was in. I was re-engineering and tailoring my philosophies and principles toward a purposeful living. Rather than the *normal* response, being angry, I was instead grateful for the challenges my neighbor had presented to me.

Exploring my options, I started volunteering my time with Big Brothers and Big Sisters in San Diego. I joined their Board of Directors and, while I was there, all of the opportunities began coming to me. I had accepted an offer to be President of the data division of a very large European telecom when, out of the blue, I received a phone call from Rage Richardson, an old high school acquaintance. He had a reality show called *Showtime* with Magic Johnson. He wanted me to handle a deal involving the famous sports agent, Leigh Steinberg.

I had two weeks before I was heading to Europe to start my new job. Therefore, I definitely was not looking for work when I went to Leigh's office to conduct this one-off business transaction. I ended up spending five hours with Leigh. The meeting went well beyond mere negotiations. Among other things, we discussed my newfound philosophies. In the midst of us talking, I noticed the striking similarities between Leigh and my brother, the rabbi, who is one year younger than me. My brother, Scott, was a Harvard genius and Leigh was a UC Berkley genius; but having found a way to communicate with my brother the genius most of my life, I was able to talk to Leigh on Leigh's level. The bottom line was that Leigh and I hit it off with Leigh texting me the next morning asking if I could return. I did, and, by the end of the day, he'd offered me the position of COO of Leigh Steinberg Sports and Entertainment.

Having secretly dreamed of being a sports agent, I accepted the job. Lest you think the newly enlightened Dave left the European telecom in the lurch, stranding people throughout the continent without phone service, don't despair. I assisted them in their search for my replacement and acted as a consultant to them for free.

I had secretly dreamed of being a sports agent, and now I was going to be with Leigh Steinberg, again the man I learned they based the movie *Jerry Maguire* on. I believe that in the same way that I had manifested Leigh, Leigh's powerful mind, which has manifested unbelievable things over the years, had manifested me. We had attracted each other, and the things we had spoken about during our initial meeting had resonated with him. It turned out that this was especially true in light of the challenging time Leigh was going through, which I was unaware of until later.

The first day that I walked into Leigh's $44,000/month space atop Fashion Island in Newport Beach, CA as his COO was surreal. My office looked out across Newport Harbor to Catalina Island and sat in between Leigh's office and Professional Hall of Fame Quarterback Warren Moon's office. Leigh had represented Warren as a player after college and, upon Warren's retirement from football, Leigh continued to represent Warren both as an announcer and in marketing opportunities. Eventually, Warren became a partner in Leigh's firm.

Once situated behind my desk, I pinched myself and then got down to business. Little did I know that my job description was about to change. Unbeknownst to me, as of Day One, I would be running all of Leigh's operations.

The day I arrived, they told me that Leigh was out sick and that, among other matters, he was in the middle of negotiations to bring a professional football team back to Los Angeles. So, along with Scott Carter, a law school intern at the time, I was promptly thrust into the middle of this huge deal with Leigh almost completely unavailable. If he did stop by the negotiations, he'd say about fifteen words (during which everyone would sit in awe of his genius because, somehow, no matter what Leigh said, people were amazed), then promptly disappear. At one point, I was able to get Leigh on the phone.

I said, "Leigh, I'm a little insecure because I have never negotiated the purchase of a billion dollar NFL team. I know you're ill, but can you give me some advice?"

There was a moment of silence, before he responded with that famous line: "Dave, my dear boy," he said. "Never negotiate to the last penny, always be fair, and don't do business with dicks."

Almost a month later, I learned that I had been talking to Leigh in rehab. No one had told me that Leigh had been arrested for public intoxication and was in court mandated alcohol rehabilitation under the threat of losing his children. I had had no idea when I had accepted Leigh's offer that he was an alcoholic.

Six months after I accepted the COO position, but had been running Leigh's business, I officially became Leigh's CEO and remained with Leigh until January 2010. Unfortunately, from the time I began until the time I left, I saw Leigh's downward spiral as his trouble with alcohol continued. It had been a twenty-year addiction with no end in sight, and he'd spent and lost millions. On the other hand, Leigh's girlfriend also struggled with dependency, but she'd successfully completed a twelve-step program. At one point, it dawned on me that when I had been in my denial, when I had been living in the world of blame, shame and justification, I'd been somewhere between Leigh and his girlfriend. I could have easily gone down the same road as Leigh.

On an extremely positive note, Leigh has now been sober for over three years, and our friendship has endured. And what I learned from Leigh while working with him, especially from his business actions, has proven invaluable. Even when intoxicated, Leigh's brilliance and wisdom shined. From him, I learned the true art of negotiation and about the spheres of influence, as will be discussed. The most important lesson he taught me, though, was about being kind to your future self. Leigh was the ultimate altruistic person. In fact, when I discuss Foundations in Section 2, Leigh's foundation at that time was not balanced, but was based mostly on humanitarian, charitable values. With his denial of his addiction now in the past, he looks to be working on building a more solid one.

In any event, at some point, Warren and I knew we wanted to work together. Maybe it was the fact that from Warren's playing days in high school through his time working with Leigh, he'd always had a short, Jewish guy by his side (I'm 5'7"). The problem was that Warren and I were both very loyal to Leigh. Then Leigh hit rock bottom in 2010.

At that point, the proverbial writing was on the wall with respect to Leigh's firm. Warren, who in addition to his responsibilities with Leigh, did and still does Seattle Seahawks' broadcasts, reached out to me in concern and flew me up to a *Monday Night Football* game in San Francisco. I brought Scott and a sports agent with me. We were in Warren's suite with him dancing around the issue for about five minutes when I finally said, "Warren, look, we're both concerned about Leigh, and you're afraid what this will do to Leigh when he finds out that you and I are going to be working together without him. But Leigh has no business. He may not even live. I need to move on."

At that time, I had had several offers from other athletes to do the exact same thing Warren and I had previously discussed – starting our own sports agency and marketing firm – but I was holding out awaiting Warren's decision.

Warren made a sad face and replied, "You're right, Dave. It's time to move on."

And so the agreement was made.

Warren offered to fund our new venture with an "obscene" amount of seed capital. I told him that I'd put together a business plan, but wanted no financing other than three months of consulting fees. This was the amount I felt was needed before I could make our new venture profitable. It turned out that I was off by two months. We became profitable one month after Sports 1 Marketing opened its doors, July 12, 2010. In fact, after the first month, I was able to pay Warren a consulting fee too.

The name "Sports 1 Marketing" was more than just a way to brand Warren. It was symbolic. All players drafted in the first round by the NFL appear on stage with the Commissioner of the NFL when announced, and their picture is taken holding the jersey of the team that selected them with the number "1" on it. It is the only time most of these guys typically are the number 1. Warren, however, wasn't drafted in the NFL. Because of the color of his skin along with his desire to play quarterback (back when black quarterbacks were virtually unheard of), he had to first play ball in Canada to prove himself. Upon his entry into the league, he chose and got to wear the number "1" throughout his long and illustrious NFL career. To me, it was the universe speaking. It was karma that Warren, the only player in both the Canadian Football Hall of Fame and the Pro Football Hall of Fame, should have his Number 1 jersey hanging proudly in Canton, Ohio.

Anyway, Warren, Scott, and I were the sole employees of Sports 1 Marketing in the early days. We did have a sports agent initially, feeling that we needed to carry over that part of Leigh's business. Within the first month, we decided that we were going to jettison the agency portion of the business and focus solely on sports marketing. Right out of the gate, our mission statement was to "Make a lot of money, help a lot of people, and have a lot of fun." I wanted to utilize this philosophy (and the Principles that I will be discussing in Section 2) as our clear objectives.

The evolution of Sports 1 Marketing has not mirrored the evolution of every business that I have ever been involved in. I have learned from my mistakes. I have employed the situational knowledge I've gained from all the previous businesses I've worked for, run, or invested in. My sole focus, my sole objectives when I wake up, are to make sure that I am in business the next day and to manifest just that by following our mission statement. Everything else becomes the proverbial cherry on top. My Principles and strategies are all about attracting and manifesting my vision, and, as long as I am able to stay in business, time is removed as a variable, and success will come. Thus, I can't provide a finite definition for Sports 1 Marketing. It will morph and change. Whatever the business is supposed to be, whatever people perceive the business to be, indeed, even whatever I perceive my business to be is, simply, what it is. We appear to have a sports and entertainment focus only because we are leveraging the two assets or resources that we have – thirty-six years of relationship capital and situational knowledge. But everything is applicable to sports and entertainment because all products, services, and companies can utilize a sports figure and a spokesperson, such as loan, drink, or energy companies.

The reality is that there are emotions around sports and entertainment, and we are able to capitalize on and maximize the monetization of those emotions by using athletes, celebrities and entertainers as "bug lights" to attract the right people to the right projects. By doing so, we raise awareness and exposure of the branding, profile building, public relations and marketing capabilities. Thus, I return to the seemingly nebulous but absolutely true definition of Sports 1 Marketing – everything in our realm is related to our reality – with the caveat so long as we are making a lot of money, helping a lot of people, and having a lot of fun.

Today, Sports 1 Marketing has fifteen full-time employees and anywhere between thirty and forty part-time employees and interns. Each year, we've been able to exponentially grow our revenue tenfold and exceed our forecasts. And, except for our two executive assistants, every employee of ours started, by design, as an intern. Our first summer, we had three interns in our program; a program that is now year-round. Presently, we have 2,500 applicants a month for 30 to 40 spots at all times. The minimum internship is a twenty hour per week commitment. We have had interns for every aspect of sports and entertainment – from accounting to public relations to marketing to graphic arts to sales to legal – and we have drawn from all over the U.S., Canada, Europe and Latin America. Most interns have come from college and graduate or professional schools, but, at times, we even have graduates, including those exploring career changes.

The interns listen in on and are actively involved with real-life business situations, thus getting practical experience. I also do trainings every week, thereby giving them an academic or classroom component that is more theoretical in nature. The interns also obtain an experience component to accompany their training by attending events that we are involved in. These events include the Super Bowl, Pro Bowl, the Masters, the Kentucky Derby, the ESPYs, the Emmys, the Oscars, and the Hall of Fame induction ceremonies, just to name a few.

For reasons that will be discussed in Section 2, the internship program is the essence of Sports 1 Marketing. Like having children to create a legacy, the internship program is the heart and soul of what we do here – of making a lot of money, helping a lot of people, and having a lot of fun. That is why we have so many applicants and put so much time, money, and effort into the program.

I've spoken to the interns about the fact that I meditate. To me, meditation is sort of the "behind the scenes" to "making a lot of money, helping a lot of people, and having a lot of fun." I've spent years in training on how to meditate, and I practice the Theta method of meditation. I wake up every morning at 4 a.m. and sit in a quiet, peaceful, comfortable place, making sure that none of my body parts are crossed. Sometimes I meditate with special meditation music, sometimes in silence, but always in darkness. I meditate at 4 a.m. because the universe has the least amount of interference around you between 2 a.m. and 4 a.m. This is when the most number of people near you are in the natural state of subconsciousness; less vibrational and standard electrical interference, and less movement is occurring. This enables you, as a medium of energy, to connect to the source faster.

I close my eyes and touch my middle fingers to my thumbs as a way to initiate the flow. I proceed to increase the vibration of my cells ten to fifty times their normal vibration rate through Theta, which is a physics state. I will actually heat up. And when I reach Theta, I know that I can manifest, be aware, and be in the flow. Thoughts will either come to or leave me in this state. But you don't ever have to reach the Theta state in order to manifest; the manifestation just won't happen as quickly. In fact, people subconsciously manifest all the time. I know this from my own personal experience.

My mom, a woman of great pride who would never ask for help, was a substitute teacher when she and my father divorced. We were broke, we lost the house, and my three siblings and I ended up living with her in a two bedroom apartment in a very bad section of town. She'd pack us our dinners, put us in an old, beat-up Country Squire station wagon, and we'd go around filling up the greeting card turnstiles at 7-11s so that we could afford to eat. Every single day, I'd tell my brothers and sister that I was going to be rich, and that I was going to buy my mom a house and a new car. This was all I thought about ... obsessively. I knew nothing about meditation at the time, but I know now that I manifested what I wanted. I believed. Let me tell you, though, it's easier to meditate than having to have gone through all that shit.

I've been asked, "How does meditation and manifesting differ from daydreaming?" Manifesting has clarity, balance and focus, as will be discussed shortly. With meditation and manifestation, I "command" the universe. "Command" here is actually defined as "working with", and you can command as small (to be grateful) or as large (for world peace) as you'd like. Daydreaming is simply allowing your subconscious to take over and letting things passively come to you. I do, however, now pay attention to my daydreams – of that passive awareness – because sometimes they eventually become something that I'll want to manifest. I now contemplate what would be best to do with the data I encounter while daydreaming.

At the end of my meditation, which occurs naturally rather than based on some sort of timing mechanism such as an alarm, I'll come back down and finish with a reaffirmation like, "It is. It shall be. It is done."

With that period now closed, I'll proceed on with my day completely clear. I may quickly go online to take notes of my meditation so I don't forget it; or motivated by what I've seen, I'll email certain people. I then send out an inspirational message of the day to a growing list of email recipients. I follow this with a rigorous workout, where I continue to process, and I actually find that things continue to come to me. One last five to ten minute computer session then takes place regarding any clarity, analysis or flow emanating from my workout before I move on to spend time with the family, eat, shower, dress, and head in to the office.

I believe that everything you've read so far lays the groundwork for and provides me with the credibility to support Section 2. As I feel I have evolved, so has my training material and what I now lecture on in my travels. I started with the solution selling system. At Compliant Company, I married solution selling with my newfound philosophy and called it "Five To Thrive". While with Leigh, I taught the interns at the office, lectured around the country, and had consulting offers to teach "Five To Thrive". This has now morphed into what follows – how to not only apply my philosophy and Principles to business, but how to also apply it to living life, thus going far beyond the selling system that I initially created.

Strap on your helmets! It's game time!

HOW TO CONNECT
TO GOODNESS

OVERVIEW

There are seven interconnected Principles that are applicable to our lives in general and just as relevant to more specific pursuits, such as business. Each of these seven Principles, in turn, I support with four components called Key Elements. The goal or objective attained in performing the Key Elements is to thrive, in a technical and spiritual sense, creating an energy that scales itself by generating its own "like-kind" energy. To demonstrate the importance of Keys, consider what you would do if a great wall impeded your path. Would you attempt to climb over it, burrow underneath it, walk all the way around it, try to blow it up? The easiest solution would be for you to find a doorway and a small Key to unlock the door in that huge wall. The point is that you don't need to spend days, weeks or years stressing over seemingly insurmountable obstacles. Instead, you'll be amazed by the great things that will open up to you by simply utilizing these Keys. You must learn how to "get out of your own way", which is another term for connecting to goodness or, as I like to define it, "source" or "source energy". I'm going to provide you with all of the Keys for life and business to help you to easily open the doors and walk right though the biggest walls or challenges that you will face.

Ultimately, we want to create a legacy where we not only put things out into the universe in a certain way that will come back to us twofold, but also where what we empower creates a similar energy. We can manifest things on an individual plane, but if we scale or empower others with our energy and create collective beliefs and collective energy, we can manifest things on a global scale, like world peace.

In a business scenario, the most successful businesses thrive by having a good portion of their marketing, advertising and sales expense incurred by others. These companies put energy out there in a specific way creating additional people (e.g., word-of-mouth) to sell for them because of the power of what they've produced and provided. Most of time, this power is defined as "exceeding expectations". When companies "exceed expectations", people preach the virtues of these companies and pass on this information. All of our best and biggest companies, like Apple, have been able to thrive utilizing the scalability of this concept.

As a broad overview, I espouse the AAA Strategy of Alignment, Action, and Adjustment; a strategy which is applicable to everything in this book as well as to life. By being more interested than interesting, I try to Align myself with everything in the universe, life, and business. In other words, I am better able to understand everything by the simple process of listening, concentrating and being aware. This enables me to focus on, and attempt to align for all concerned, the reasons for wanting to do something or not; the impact it will have, and my and perhaps others' capabilities. Assuming alignment, I am now able to take Action. Later in this book, I will teach you how to create a "success criteria", which will enable you to exceed the expectations of anyone you are dealing with. But I have learned through my situational knowledge and experiences that life doesn't stop there, and I always need to be prepared for the most important element: Adjustment. One of my favorite sayings is, "If you want to make God laugh, create a well-developed plan." Shit happens, and we are not in control. The universe will, in fact, be laughing at me if I think that I can control it.

In order to adhere to the AAA Strategy, we need to utilize and understand the 80/20/80 Rule, which I will be discussing in greater depth later. Basically, though, the greatest chance of statistical success in life and in business will come from spending 80% of your time planning and aligning and 20% of your time putting that plan into action. At that point, within that action, you flip this equation and spend 20% of your time actually taking the action itself and 80% of your time adjusting by managing the tangentials and exceeding whatever expectations others have with respect to that action.

But I can, through my AAA Strategy, ultimately align with the universe and make a non-corroded, true connection with source or goodness leading to fast and accurate manifestation of anything I desire. Keep in mind, though, that there is a balance in the universe; expended energy needs to be replaced, and the more energy we release as "energy vessels", the more energy we get back. So, in the same way source can lead to a positive manifestation, we also have the power to manifest a negative energy that we may not mean to bring upon ourselves. For example, do you ever feel disconnected or have negative thoughts or chatter in your head? Of course you do. When this happens I simply say, "Cancel!" out loud or to myself. This is what I meant by "getting out of my own way". "Cancel" negates the negative energy – those negative thoughts, worries, concerns and the like – before they grow arms and legs and manifests what I don't desire … "Cancel".

Remember, these Principles and their supporting Key Elements are interconnected. Like life itself, nothing exists in a vacuum, and I have labeled and categorized the Seven Principles and their supporting Four Key Elements for your convenience.

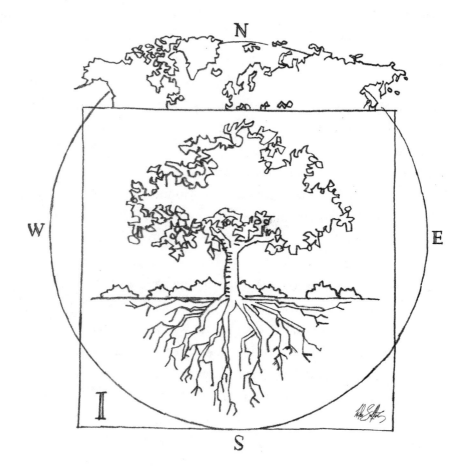

I. PRINCIPLE ONE: FOUNDATION

"He who has not first laid his foundations may be able with great ability to lay them afterwards, but they will be laid with trouble to the architect and danger to the building."

Niccolo Machiavelli

Everything in life, from the construction of a building to a relationship, requires a solid foundation, or it will crumble. If certain things are not in place, you'll not be able to support all of the other things you wish to accomplish. We want that foundation and support to be solid. We want that foundation and support to be concrete with steel rods, not balsa wood. We want to create the best foundation in order to manifest things faster and more accurately.

Values provide that foundation. No matter what you attract in your life, identify, prioritize, and utilize your own values to build the foundation that best will provide clarity, balance and focus with confidence. Confidence in what you're trying to manifest will attract what you desire.

PERSONAL	EXPERIENCE	GIVING	RECEIVING

FOUNDATION PRINCIPLE – KEY ELEMENT #1: PERSONAL VALUES

When you are manifesting your vision, you need to analyze the effect on your personal values. Personal values are the most valuable of your assets. These include integrity, character, honesty, discipline, and work ethic to name a few. But as the name implies, these values will be personal to you based on your own perception and prioritized as such and, naturally, will differ from person to person. In other words, you have your distinct personal values and I have my own. Still, these are the values that you identify, prioritize and build a solid foundation on. When you are manifesting your intentions ask how will this affect your personal values? Then continue to balance the other Key Element values that follow. Utilize the AAA Strategy to align, take action and adjust accordingly to manifest what best connects you to source or goodness.

> "I respect the man who knows distinctly what he wishes. The greater part of all mischief in the world arises from the fact that men do not sufficiently understand their own aims. They have undertaken to build a tower, and spend no more labor on the foundation than would be necessary to erect a hut."
> Johann Wolfgang von Goethe

Again, "source" is God, Jesus, Buddha, the Universe, or whatever it is you want to call it, and it is the only thing out there that has no equal and opposite. Simply stated source is goodness. I believe in the physics and dynamics of the universe and, to that end, draw a lot from those individuals who have studied the universe and have made discoveries or presented theories that resonate with me. For instance, one of my mentors is Max Planck, the Nobel prize-winning German theoretical physicist who originated quantum theory. This theory revolutionized human understanding of atomic and subatomic properties. Max Planck stated:

> "All matter originates and exists only by virtue of a force
> which brings the particle of an atom to vibration and holds

this most minute solar system of the atom together. We must assume behind this force the existence of a conscious and intelligent mind. This mind is the matrix of all matter."

This quote can be interpreted many ways, but to me, this "force" that interconnects everyone and everything is source or goodness, and this interconnection affects everything from life itself to more specific categories, such as business.

Returning to personal values, a book I strongly recommend reading is Sun Tzu's *Art of War.* Sun Tzu's philosophies can be taken on many levels, are especially useful in life and business, and are extremely enlightening. Initially, Sun Tzu states: "He who is cowardly can be captured." Courage is an important personal value because it manifests confidence. Someone who projects insecurity or takes a position of fear will attract more fear or more of the wrong things, and will not be successful. Clarity, balance and focus brings confidence; and someone who is confident is not cowardly and will thus attract more positive energy.

> "If you have built castles in the air, your work need not be lost; that is where they should be. Now put the foundations under them."
>
> Henry David Thoreau

True courage is believing in yourself – being you – and being fine with that. I always say, "It is better to be hated for who you are than loved for who you are not."

I used to be one of those people who wanted to please everyone and make everyone happy. But I've learned that in trying to please everyone, you end up pleasing no one. Be it in life or business, you end up spreading yourself too thin and resentment follows. For example, when I'd go to the Super Bowl, I'd try to get everyone else tickets and VIP passes, which are difficult to obtain. I never promised that I could get the tickets and passes, but the people with me had such high expectations that they were resentful if I couldn't come through.

I ended up worrying about everyone else and not having a good time myself.

Instead, make your goal "to connect to goodness and be happy". This will attract happiness to you which, in turn, will make everyone else happy. Have the courage to be who you want to be and to adhere to all of your values; especially your personal values, and you'll manifest faster and more accurately what you desire. Be courageous and express your opinions and ideas honestly.

Another lesson from Sun Tzu is "He who is quick tempered can be insulted." Therefore, there is a need to focus on staying connected to goodness and not letting our egos get in our way. This is a very important personal value for being centered and at peace. Just as you need the courage to be you, you also need to be able to control your emotions and shift your energy when you get disconnected from source or goodness. For example, if you try to insult me, I allow you to have your opinion, but I don't respond with negative energy. Instead, I silently pray for your happiness and walk away. The universe is abundant, and if someone does not like something about me, I simply don't give it any energy.

> "Everyone values things differently. In other words, they place their own value on everything that affects their lives. Also from moment to moment they may even change their values. Such as a person, who values diamonds above all else, might be willing to trade a gallon of diamonds for a drink of water to save his life in a desert. What this means is value is a relative thing depending on a need or a perceived need. Yet, how many people will argue and even violently fight over the perceived value of something or some idea only later have an entirely different view point or value."
>
> Sidney Madwed

However, when our family members tell us their opinions or let us know what they think we should do, we typically find ourselves extremely challenged to stay connected to source. But as someone once taught me: "God gave us friends to apologize for our families." In all seriousness, family members generally mean well and are trying to manifest for us what they think is in our best interest; after all, family creates our first and core collective beliefs. In response, we quite often want their approval and acceptance – especially for those of you with Jewish or Catholic mothers; remember: the Jews may have invented guilt, but the Catholics perfected it. Unfortunately, when our well-intentioned mothers or family members suggest or try to determine our future, it can sometimes prove destructive to our values. Instead of being pure to ourselves and connected to source, we're being pure to something and somebody else. Thus, we are not aligned with the action and manifestation that we're looking for. One of the first times I went against my family's expectation was when I took the job out of law school with West Publishing over a position with the D.A.'s office in New Jersey. My family's general comment was: "So, you're not going to be a *real* lawyer?" (spoken with a Yiddish accent). No one seemingly supported me in my decision, and yet this decision, *my* decision, proved to be one of the most beneficial experiences of my life.

> "Character is what you have left when you've lost everything you can lose."
> Evan Esar

Personally, the older I get, the more I try to stay in a "majesty of calmness". That is, I try to stay connected to source and at peace.

Additionally, Sun Tzu teaches: "He who is moral can be shamed." What does this mean? He means live "above the line" in a state of "Accountability", instead of like most people who live in a state of "Blame, Shame and Justification". They blame others, they are shameful for their actions and/or they justify what they do instead of taking Accountability for what they've attracted in their lives. I need to be me and you need to be you, but I don't need to place myself on a pedestal, nor do you. Stay within yourself. Do not blame others, do not be shameful of your opinions or mistakes, and there is definitely no need to justify your beliefs or opinions to anyone. Don't profess your morality. Don't preach how great and perfect you are. Keep your ego in check, and have a sense of reality and security that it is okay to be human. It is okay to make mistakes. I look for progress, not perfection. Everyone has their vices. In the end, we are the sum (both good and bad) of who we are.

> "Every saint has a past and every sinner has a future."
> Oscar Wilde

Similarly, others are who they are, but in the same way only you can be responsible for yourself; they, alone, need to be responsible for themselves. Before you accuse me of callousness, let me explain. Have you ever felt better because someone felt badly for you? I am not talking about empathy. Empathy is someone caring about or aligning with your feelings. If one of my children hurts his – or herself, I feel it, I cringe, I wish I was the one who was hurt. This is different from feeling sorry for someone in a bad position. You cannot feel bad enough for someone to make them feel better. You cannot be confused enough to help someone get clarity. You cannot be sad enough to make someone happy. You cannot be hungry enough to help feed someone. But the more you pray for someone's happiness and put out positive energy, the better they will feel. In order to heal or help, you need to create energy in a diverse or reactive manner. Put out the energy you want for others, but most importantly take care of yourself; the stronger your connection to source or goodness, the more you can create abundance for all.

FOUNDATION PRINCIPLE – KEY ELEMENT #2: EXPERIENCE VALUES

The Second Key Element is Experience Values, and this is also a very important matter to consider when we are creating balance in our lives or business. This includes all of your experiences, your situational knowledge, and your education. Our experience includes both our success and failures. In fact, our failures can be our greatest assets if we can learn something from them and move forward. Learning from our experiences ensures that we don't pay the "dummy tax" again. And, clearly, the older we are, the more experiences, situational knowledge and education we have to draw from. How valuable is our experience? Just ponder what it would be like to forget everything you know and have to start all over.

> "Experience is the name everyone gives to their mistakes."
>
> Oscar Wilde

But in order for you to learn, you must make mistakes. That is the only way you will be able to learn and gain experience ... experience does matter, especially in business. For instance, once you've worked for twenty years within a corporate bureaucracy and understand the systematic values of each manager and director, and have sat on corporate boards, you'll be an invaluable asset to just about any corporation or business.

There is no substitute for experience. Not only do we learn from our own experience, but I find it extremely valuable to learn from others' experiences. This is another example of why it is so important to be more interested than interesting. I try to spend as much time as I can with highly experienced people; I want to learn from them so I don't have to pay the "dummy tax" they've paid.

I used to talk to both of my grandfathers every week through the time I graduated law school. I attribute a lot of my early success to these conversations and the Q & As we had. For example, the basis for my focused life and business objectives came from my Poppa Marty. Recall from Section 1, he was the one who told me that you only need three things to be fulfilled in life. First, find one partner in life that you truly love. He/She will be the liaison between you and your family. Because you spend 1/3 of your life with your family, you need the right partner to have a fulfilled family life. Second, find the

> "If history repeats itself, and the unexpected always happens, how incapable must Man be of learning from experience?"
>
> George Bernard Shaw

one job you love. You spend 1/3 of your life working, so you need to love what you do. Finally, as for the final 1/3, find the best bed you can. Poppa Marty explained with a wink, "It's because you spend 1/3 of your life sleeping and shtupping." (Yiddish for sex)

It's the challenges, the struggles, the successes and failures that make me who I am today. Appreciate all of your experiences, and learn from them in order to stay connected to source and goodness.

Foundation Principle – Key Element #3: Giving Values

The philanthropic component of Key Element #3: Giving Values is the essence of the universe and source…Abundance. As John Donne said, "No man is an island." I truly believe in the laws of the universe. Everyone and Everything is interconnected, and you need to ask, "How am I contributing and outwardly directing positive energy? How will this affect others around me? What have I given to the universe?"

> "In charity there is no excess."
> Sir Francis Bacon

Quantum physics has shown that everything vibrates. The earth and its minerals vibrate the slowest, trees and plants next, followed by animals and humans who vibrate the fastest. We can only be aware of those things which vibrate equal to or slower than us, but the interconnection between everything and everyone still exists. Something that affects plants and animals will, in some way, affect us in the same way that cutting off just one branch of a tree will affect that tree, maybe even leading to that tree's eventual death. We need to understand that we're all connected to source and, therefore, have an accountability to ourselves that then connects to others as well.

One of my favorite adages is simply: "What you give, you will get back or receive." You need the same energy for both giving and receiving. It is not good to always receive. Likewise, it is not good to always give. Within the realm of physics, unless you have a balance, you create instability. So, be aware of your own energy of giving and receiving. You need to balance your values and stay connected with the flow of energy.

For example, when I first started making money, I was not as connected to source. I felt insecure that all the abundance I was receiving was not going to last. I was afraid to spend the money I earned too freely for fear that it would not keep coming. I eventually became more confident and less scarcity-minded. Unfortunately, I then became too overly-generous and forgot that it is not only important to give, but equally important to receive. I started to give practically everything I had to everyone. For example, I could not go out to eat without picking up the check. I felt obligated to empty my vessel, but wouldn't allow the universe to refill it. I went from a paucity in giving to a paucity of receiving to such an extent that it would bother me or be almost insulting if someone else would pay for me or buy me a gift.

Also related to my "giving" issues was the inherent feeling that I was responsible or obligated to anyone who'd supported or helped me throughout my journey. People came

> "With malice toward none, with charity for all ... let us strive on to finish the work we are in ... to do all which may achieve and cherish a just and lasting peace among ourselves and with all nations."
>
> Abraham Lincoln

out of the woodwork to ask for my help, mostly financially in the way of loans. Unfortunately, I just could not say "No" when what I should have said is I would "work with them to help them". I became an enabler to my friends and family and lost millions of dollars. Just the act of having to ask me for help or the inability to pay me back, forced most of my friends and family to go "below the line" into blame, shame and justification and put an obvious strain on many of my relationships.

I developed what I call the "Puppy Dog Syndrome"; I had to take every puppy dog in and save it. Sun Tzu wrote: "He who is fond of people can be worried." To me, this relates most to this "Giving" Value. We create energy out of abundance. We don't "do for others" for a specific return. We "do for others" to manifest what we desire individually and collectively. We give in order to connect to source or goodness. Be careful, though, as benevolence itself and a fondness of other people can create the energy of worry or responsibility. In business, many people who make a lot of money fail because of benevolence; they feel too responsible for other people. It's very difficult when you're a good, caring person to understand the difference between generosity and carrying an energy with you that you are responsible for everyone. Again, it is not a selfish thing for me to tell you that you're only responsible for yourself. As long as you live connected to goodness, others will benefit from this power as well.

For example, my mom spent forty-seven years teaching at her starting salary of $17,000 a year. She gave everything she could to her six children and her students, as a catalyst for all of them to thrive. But she was always worried and shamed because she wasn't

> Charity sees the need not the cause.
> German Proverb

taking care of herself. In the end, she lost credibility and energy because others had to help her. If she'd focused that energy, stimulation and capacity initially on herself, she'd have created that same abundance for her children and students, but also would've been whole herself. In fact, in my "loving" (remember, my mom will read this book and I still can't completely rid myself of my wanting to please her) opinion, she'd have been even more successful and abundant by taking care of herself and putting her energy into who she was; all of those other things would've ultimately thrived as well.

Because this is counterintuitive, it's a hard concept to come to terms with. In my case, it was a challenge to think that I wasn't responsible for my mom ... nor my wife, my children, nor anyone else besides myself. By being responsible for myself within my personal values, I trust the universe and know that everyone will benefit if I stay connected to source and goodness. You will drain yourself of energy, and you'll be able incapable of creating the abundance for others by feeling responsible for them. Put yourself first and others will benefit. Trust me, when you create abundance and connect to goodness you will affect all others with your positive energy. This giving value is equally applicable to the workplace. As mentioned, we have interns at Sports 1 Marketing. In the business deals they work on, I could certainly do a better, faster job. So from a purely short-term monetary standpoint, I lose money on each deal they work on. But this is not my objective or intention. My long-term perspective with interns is

> "If you don't have solid beliefs you cannot build a stable life. Beliefs are like the foundation of a building, and they are the foundation to build your life upon."
>
> Alfred A. Montapert

to work with and develop these young people, provide them with insight and an experience I define as "situational knowledge". Remember, this is one-third of what I love to do – help other people. Thus, there is a giving and receiving or flow of energy in both directions.

The internship program also falls under the auspices of my mentor Leigh Steinberg's theory of "being kind to your future self". By understanding that we need to stay connected to source and goodness eventually these 18 – 22 year olds will be running businesses and sports teams. If you are the impetus and catalyst that helped create this for them, you are "being kind to your future self" in creating that scalability of energy or perpetuating your manifestations as a collective energy or belief. In twenty years, you will be able to turn to these now executives, in all fields of business ranging from ticket sales to team owners, who you have empowered to become successful, purposeful people to in turn help you. The hope is that you've provided these mostly inexperienced, young people at an early stage with your relationship capital and situational knowledge. It is your intention that someday the recipient going forward of their appreciation will be you and your business.

However, for those who continue at Sports 1 Marketing after their internship, they can also directly join me in my three pursuits – having lots of fun, and making lots of money – and yes, helping others themselves. What allows me to thrive is when they thrive, and I can focus and train even more people to create more positive energy that I intend to scale as collective positive beliefs or energy.

> "The ultimate determinant in the struggle now going on for the world will not be bombs and rockets but a test of wills and ideas – a trial of spiritual resolve: the values we hold, the beliefs we cherish and the ideals to which we are dedicated."
>
> Ronald Reagan

Finally, in what is usually my last act of giving before large numbers of interns end their internships with us and head back to school, I share with them the following advice. I believe it to be highly relevant in today's work and marketplace. So my ultimate gift to my interns is to empower them with energy and personal and experience values so that they in turn can empower others.

PERSONAL VALUE: Time is infinite, but limited. This paradox is very difficult for young professionals to comprehend. On the one hand, time is infinite, and we must be patient for the universe to give us the right thing at the right time. On the other hand, we only have 24 hours in a day, and we must use them most efficiently, effectively, and be as statistically successful as we can with great urgency.

EXPERIENCE VALUE: Great ability is not enough! Remember, there is no need for accolades or recognition of achievement. You can't rest on your previous successes. You are not as good as they say you are. Ability can only take you so far. So keep striving to thrive for all you hope to manifest more accurately and rapidly.

EXPERIENCE VALUE: We need to reset our lives with the right momentum… so wake up early! Imagine each day is like a big street hill in San Francisco and each morning you are at the top peak of that hill with just one hand on your car to keep it from rolling down the hill. Now imagine trying to stop the car at the end of the day at the bottom of the hill. You need to wake up early to create the right momentum because trying to create or change your momentum at the end of the day would be like attempting to stop the car at the bottom of the steep hill with that one hand.

EXPERIENCE VALUE: Talk to people. Likes attract likes. Words are much more powerful when spoken! They vibrate faster and will attract what you desire faster! Don't be afraid when you discover that talking to people is not only much more effective and statistically successful than texting or emailing, it is a lot more fun … and feeling good is our ultimate objective!

PERSONAL VALUE: Be the First to Arrive and the Last to Revive. Get noticed and be more productive. In order to get 64 hours of production in a day, you must be the first to arrive and the last person to leave. You have a lot to do in a day, and statistically you will produce so much more if you work twice the hours of the average Joe. Trust me, you will get what you give – the universe guarantees it!

PERSONAL VALUE: Be proactive to attract what you desire. Do not wait for others to tell you what you or they want. Be accountable! Do not live below the line in blame, shame and justification. The "waiting game" will not help you manifest what your desire more accurately or rapidly. Being proactive will also help you shine and get noticed.

PERSONAL VALUE: Make mistakes, but be accountable. You need to be living in the "learning zone" and making a lot of mistakes! As such, you need to continually expand your "comfort zone", and in order to do this successfully, you need to be accountable and learn from each mistake. In this way, your new "comfort zone" emerges from your previous "learning zone" and fairly soon everything formerly "foreign" will now seem easy!

EXPERIENCE VALUE: Constructive criticism is necessary. Work for people who have high standards! Work for the best who demand the best! Don't cheat yourself by working for pre-school teachers. Work for the people who demand the most! You will not know what you are capable of unless you push yourself, and most importantly, you are pushed by others for greatness.

EXPERIENCE VALUE: Break through the surface. Follow through and see things to their end. You can't quit every job when it gets tough, or you don't agree with the "powers that be". Too many young professionals forget that they need to not only build skills sets of what, when, and how to be successful, but they also need to take the time to break through the surface and obtain titled positions and experience in order to make lateral moves! If you keep jumping jobs, you are cheating yourself and will wonder why you are still at an entry level position after so many years.

PERSONAL VALUE: Fur over Fluff. Remember, just because a blanket is fluffy doesn't mean it's warm. Choose a company with substance. Make sure it is financially stable and built with the right leadership, character, and situational knowledge. X-box and candy may be fun, but they just won't get it done!

EXPERIENCE VALUE: Manifest what you want more accurately and rapidly. Meditate each morning on what you want and be willing to put enough energy out in the universe to attract it. Remember, your free will should be used to connect to goodness, so do whatever it takes. No job is beneath you, and your positive attitude and awareness will help you stay focused to manifest exactly what you desire!

PERSONAL VALUE: No need to be offended or to offend. You must share your vision and help others manifest to theirs. You can not be offended when you hear others talking about you! You also must do your best to not offend others. Speak the truth, and the truth will be spoken about you. Unfortunately, too many people get caught up chatting negatively to others, or in the alternative, too many of us listen to our own negative chatter.

EXPERIENCE VALUE: Connect to goodness. Make your relationships deep and meaningful. It's not only what you know, but who you know that matters. Make as many relationships with power sponsors and decision makers as possible. If you connect to these people using the Ben Franklin effect, you will find that you will manifest what you desire much more rapidly.

EXPERIENCE VALUE: Surround yourself with the circumstance you desire. Surround yourself with the people, places and things you desire. Make sure you choose the best mentors who have the attributes that you desire and value what you value. Remember likes attract likes, so be part of the "nth" Power and be empowered by those people you most want to emulate. Find the right crowd!

EXPERIENCE VALUE: If it is too good to be true … It is! This simple lesson is so hard to live by and so simple to understand. Trust the universe. If it doesn't feel right, it is not right. I promise you that 100% of the time, if something is too good to be true…it is! Remind yourself of this every time your emotions take control and your ego tries to convince you otherwise. Remember the parable about the Tortoise and the Hare!

Utilizing Key Element #3 Giving Values, the gift of empowerment is the most important energy we can impart. Yes, give your positive energy to others, so they in turn can share it with others. These "parting shots" for my interns will create a legacy I am proud of and, most importantly, will help me and others make a lot of money, help a lot of people, and have a lot of fun.

FOUNDATION PRINCIPLE – KEY ELEMENT #4: RECEIVING VALUES

The fourth Key Element under the Principle of Foundation is Receiving Values. This is the wealth element and, in my opinion, although many people may not initially agree, it is the least important of the Four Key Elements or values. I've heard everything possible about money – from having more money makes everything easier – to my favorite money quote: "Money can't buy you love, but it sure rents the shit out of it." Wealth is certainly something to strive for, but to reiterate, there must be a balance of all four of these Key Elements under the Principle of Foundation. Many wealthy individuals are unhappy, physically ill, or have shallow relationships, failing to take care of their personal values. All the money in the world cannot bring back their quality of life. They do not understand enlightenment, fulfillment or balance. Wayne Dyer (one of my spiritual gurus) stated, "There is no way to happiness … Happiness is the way."

> "Poor is the man who does not know his own intrinsic worth and tends to measure everything by relative value. A man of financial wealth who values himself by his financial net worth is poorer than a poor man who values himself by his intrinsic self-worth."
>
> Sidney Madwed

The irony is that most individuals just starting out focus solely on their financial values. The mindset becomes one of "If only I had this one Key Element in my life – the money to pay off this student loan, or buy this or that, have some spending money – I would be all set and happy." Sadly, the worry over this last value then carries throughout life as the primary focus. How will I save money? How will I make my money grow? How will I divide my money? How will I dispose of my money? The universe does not understand scarcity or lack. So, when you focus on what you don't have enough of, the universe will bring you more of what you are lacking.

The reality is that even if you are financially bankrupt, if you focus on the other three values – personal, experience, and giving – you will become fulfilled and the financial element will fall into place if you are ready to receive. Your financial value is a renewable resource. You can always make back the money, but not the other three values. Without the first three values, those wealthy individuals, regardless of how they obtained that wealth, do not know how to make it back. This is why I truly believe that if you took all of the wealth in the world and put it in one spot, it would redistribute itself to the same people who understand the interrelationship of these values. These same people create their own abundance. It is akin to those people who will themselves to stay healthy. For the most part, they do stay healthy. It's the old mind over matter principle.

> "Your most precious possession is not your financial assets. Your most precious possession is the people you have working there, and what they carry around in their heads, and their ability to work together."
>
> Robert Reich

The only reason that money is even a value of mine, beyond to keep my receiving energy balanced with my giving energy, is because money is a form of energy. It has its own reality of vibration which provides me with the ability to help a lot of people and have a lot of fun. I've learned that the more money I have the more people I can help and the more fun I can have. I was inspired by my mom as a catalyst for positive change, dedicating her entire life to helping and teaching others. My perspective differed only in that I wanted to create such abundance that I could afford to give a hundred people like my mom opportunities. I believe that my having the ability to hire one hundred teachers would be more beneficial to the universe than simply me, one person, teaching … although I believe I can do both!

Again, to sum it up, please don't lose sleep or waste your energy in regards to money. Don't let it drive you. Let your driving force be clarity, balance, focus and confidence based on your personal, experience and humanitarian values because the money will come based on what you want to manifest as long as you remain ready to receive. Remember, as Wayne Dyer taught me, "Change the way you look at things, and the things you look at change." If you are worried and focused in on not having enough, that is what the universe is going to bring you – not enough. If you believe in scarcity and your own self-interest, then that is what you will manifest. But if you truly believe in the universe, if you truly believe in abundance, then there is enough of everything for everyone. If you stay connected to source and create abundance, you will attract what you desire more accurately and rapidly.

> "I'm the only person I know that's lost a quarter of a billion dollars in one year... It's very character-building."
>
> Steve Jobs

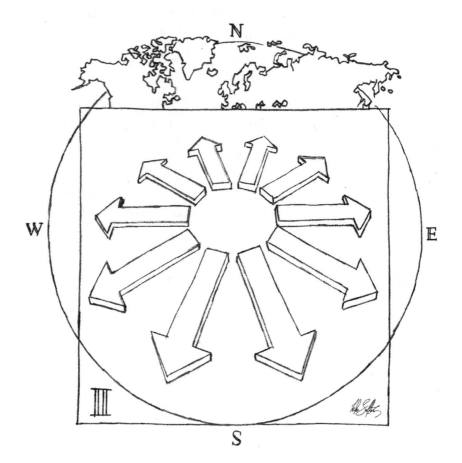

II. PRINCIPLE TWO: GUIDEPOSTS

"Clarity of mind means clarity of passion, too; this is why a great and clear mind loves ardently and sees distinctly what it loves."

Blaise Pascal

"The best and safest thing is to keep a balance in your life, acknowledge the great powers around us and in us. If you can do that, and live that way, you are really a wise man."

Euripides

The foundation of Values is crucial, but you then need to fortify that foundation. Both theoretically and spiritually, guideposts provide that fortification. These, like Foundation and the five remaining Principles, can be broken down into four Key Elements. No matter what you attract in your life, utilize guideposts to fortify your foundation by way of clarity, balance, and focus. Having clarity, balance, and focus will, in turn, give you confidence. Moreover, clarity will create velocity, balance will create stability, and focus will create accuracy. With velocity, stability, and accuracy, you will attract what you desire much faster – painlessly and seamlessly – while getting out of your own way, being in the flow of energy, and connected to goodness.

Guidepost Principle – Key Element #1: Clarity

Have you ever been in a personal or business situation where you thought you understood what was going on only to gain clarity later as to what the situation was all about, and it was nothing like you perceived it to be? You must be clear on what you want in order to create the velocity to put through your new value-based stable foundation.

And what is velocity? This is the energy expended in stimulating the universe, which creates the efficiency of attracting. It is utilizing the abundant power of the universe in the most efficient manner to manifest and attract those things you desire faster by being connected to source, or "in the flow". What is the flow of energy or being connected? Have you ever been on a basketball court and every shot from every angle you've put up has gone in? Being in "the zone" is the sports analogy to being "in the flow". When you're in the flow of the universe, you just know it. You are in harmony and peace with the universe.

When we talk about clarity in a broad sense, I know the three things I want out of my day, as articulated earlier – today, I want to make a lot of money, help a lot of people, and have a lot of fun. So if something happens in my day where I'm not making or working toward these objectives of having fun, making a lot of money, or helping people, I take a second to shift my energy. I take a moment to myself in order to change my perspective. What most people lose sight of and yet what we are really

> "Knowledge, without common sense," says Lee, is "folly; without method, it is waste; without kindness, it is fanaticism; without religion, it is death. But with common sense, it is wisdom with method, it is power; with clarity, it is beneficence; with religion, it is virtue, and life, and peace."
>
> Austin Farrar

searching for in a purposeful existence is peace. At peace, you will manifest what you desire faster and more accurately.

In a business sense, clarity allows us to stimulate interest, just as clarity allows us to create velocity or stimulate the universe. I define stimulating interest in a business context as creating curiosity with a clearly defined objective. In business we are, naturally, creating curiosity in regards to that deal or sale, and the clearly defined objective is generally getting the person to move forward to the next step in the process. And how do you even take that first step to stimulate interest?

I have a proven theory that in one day, I can send a person, trained by me, to a hotel lobby or pool or a trade show and they will do more business than anyone

> "It's a lack of clarity that creates chaos and frustration. Those emotions are poison to any living goal."
>
> Steve Maraboli

sitting in my office making calls all day. This is because it is better to get out and meet people, creating a direct connection to stimulate their interest. In my opinion, this is the best mechanism to attract with confidence. Trade shows, in particular, are great venues. Look at the number of business sponsors, business booths, and attendees there are at trade shows.

Breakfast clubs, Chambers of Commerce, Small Business Administrations, Golf Courses, Social Events, Trips are all potential places to make connections, but the full list of where you can meet people goes on and on. My wife hates this, but I usually walk away from weddings with at least three or four business cards. Not every social situation, however, needs to be all social in the same way that not every business situation has to be all business. They can overlap one another. It also doesn't have to be torture. Go to those places where you'd go anyway and continue to do what you like to do. In fact, you'll often connect more quickly at these places because there will be some sort of commonality. Everything is connected in our universe.

We want to attract and connect to as many "like kind" people as we can. This is what I call "relationship capital". Creating relationship capital and learning how to leverage it is important in all businesses and life. Half of my business value is derived from this asset I call relationship capital! Networking works. *Who* you know matters more than *what* you know. It exposes and attracts opportunities. The more people you can expose to what you do by getting the word out on the value and energy of your business, the greater the likelihood that someone of "like mind" may be attracted and will contact you. Statistically, a ballplayer with thirty at bats is more likely to get three hits than a player

> "If you have zest and enthusiasm you attract zest and enthusiasm. Life does give back in kind."
>
> Norman Vincent Peale

who only gets ten at bats, even if the person with thirty at bats is only half as good. It is simple math!

Everywhere you go, connect … smile, make eye contact, meet and talk to people. Be more interested than interesting, smile, ask them, "How are you?" … then make sure you listen for and acknowledge their answer!

Listening is the most underutilized skill in life and business. As my grandmother used to say, "Why do you think God gave us two ears and only one mouth?" I absolutely agree that you should be listening twice as much as you are speaking. So, follow up your first question with "Where are you from?", "What are you doing here?" or "What do you do?" Remember, what is a person's favorite thing to talk about?… Themselves! Each person's story is what excites them most. The more we listen, the greater our awareness becomes, and the more we can align, take action, and adjust. After all, as the old adage says, "Better to remain silent and be thought a fool than to speak out and remove all doubt" – and old adages are still around for a reason.

Additionally, don't forget to grab business cards. I take every business card I can and put them in our database. I've offered incentives to my employees and interns to pick up business cards. Taking someone's card is an initial way to make a connection, which increases the statistical success of attracting them to our business or vision. I also want as many people in my database as possible because I do many mass emails to this database including, but not limited to, our professionally produced Monthly Newsletter, *Around the Moon*. The more people who are exposed to what we are involved with, the more people who will be attracted to and stimulated by what we're doing. Just like in my baseball analogy, the more at bats we get, the more statistically

> "More important than the quest for certainty is the quest for clarity."
> Francois Gautier

successful we will be! In other words, we can make more money, help more people, and have more fun! The more people you connect with the faster and more accurately you can manifest what you desire.

Naturally, thinking or generating those powerful mental waves of energy is also a great way to expose opportunities within the universe. The more time you take to think and connect, the more clarity with velocity you will create. Don't simply act or react. Before you go to the lobby or the pool, or make a phone call, think for a second: "Okay, exactly what is my clear objective and what result do I want to manifest?"

For example, we knew that we were producing a baseball movie with acclaimed filmmaker Sean Pamphilion, producer, writer and director of *The United States of Football*, which had the second largest theatrical release for a sports documentary ever and *Run, Ricky, Run* for ESPN's *30 for 30* series and award-winning writer, producer and director Richard "Rick" Cohen (*Faded Glory, Season of a Lifetime*).

Our clear objective was to find sponsors for the film, and we would offer product placement in the movie in exchange for product and $50,000.

In contemplating this objective, we considered the reasons someone would have to want to do it, the impact this would have on their company, and the capabilities that we have in order to create value for them. *Baseball Digest*, the oldest baseball magazine resource in the U.S., was one of the companies we thought to approach. We asked for copies and "give away" promotional items for product placement use (it would be used as a prop in the film with ballplayers reading copies of the magazine in the dugout or on the plane), and we'd provide them with all of this value for $50,000.

> "Simplicity, clarity, singleness: these are the attributes that give our lives power and vividness and joy."
>
> Richard Halloway

Because of the short timing and *Baseball Digest's* business model, they didn't have a $50,000 budget. Returning to the reasons, impacts, and capabilities, we were able to create a mutually beneficial arrangement where we would receive $100,000 of front cover advertising for this film plus another project, a film festival, which we were involved in. And not only could we utilize the value of the exposure for the film and film festival, but we could use it for other contributing companies' product placements. This created exponential value, allowing us to close twice as many deals and generate ten times the revenue. *Baseball Digest*, on the other hand, received the product placement opportunity as well as our agreement to distribute their magazine at several key events, including the film festival.

This is an example of a situation of everybody being abundant despite us not receiving the hard cost we were initially seeking. In fact, by staying connected to goodness and not force feeding what I initially thought would be the reasons leading to a sponsorship, we ended up with an even more abundant opportunity. I was able to share a vision with the correct value so they had no resistance. I was able to list of all the capabilities we had that added supplemental value so that the value index exceeded their expectations and allowed them to make a reasonable counter proposal (whereas, in the case of other companies, finding the necessary budget may have been the ultimate result).

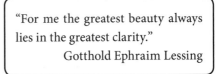

"For me the greatest beauty always lies in the greatest clarity."
Gotthold Ephraim Lessing

Whenever possible on my business calls or in meetings, I will summarize the conversation and conclude with, "Does that sound fair?" I will have summarized the reasons someone will be doing something, the impacts it will have, and the capabilities I have to create value. By asking the simple question, "Does that sound fair?" a soft commitment or agreement always follows.

I truly believe in fairness in business as well as in life. I believe that most people seek fairness. That is why fairness is one of the three things that Leigh advised me on in making unilateral business decisions. Recall from the Preface to this book, Leigh instructed me, "Never negotiate to the last penny, ALWAYS BE FAIR, and don't do business with DICKS!"

If most human beings weren't so innately sensitive to this concept, why is one of the favorite statements of our children, "That's not fair!"? (Of course, I tell my kids that the only "fair" I know of is where you can enter a pig or cow, and go on rides) But there is an emotional tie or element to fairness, and if you can get alignment or agreement with someone that something is fair, it transcends any economic value or interest; and people will statistically then perform as promised. Fairness is an energy that you want to generate in your life as well as an energy you want to attract. As a simple example, I will have greater statistical success if I say, "So you will call me on Tuesday?

Does that sound fair?" than if someone says to me, "I'll call you back" or if I say, "Do you promise to call me back on Tuesday?" There is an energized, cemented commitment to this simple thing asked in the first instance that is less prone to resistance than in the second or third. If people agree to be fair, they are more apt to do so. A commitment of fairness is a great start to everything else that will follow.

In determining what will be fair to you, you need to project what it is that you want to manifest. You need to define your objectives. Use as a basis the effects on your own foundation or values so that everything becomes easier in making your decision, thus avoiding any gray areas. For example, when you meditate or focus on what you desire, project that you want big opportunities, no resistance, and success. The energies of all of your phone calls will then be

> "He talked with more claret than clarity."
>
> Susan Ertz

exactly what you put out there. I've heard people who work for me say, "I haven't called this prospect yet because I like to make the hard calls last." I respond, "Cancel that negative thought. There is nothing hard. We will face no resistance and this will be the first call that we'll make."

I like to prioritize things by importance and not be fooled by "urgent" less important things. For example, during my trainings I ask my staff at Sports 1 Marketing to raise their hands if they would give something "urgent" priority over something that was "important" and, inevitably, over 90% raise their hands. I believe in the exact opposite. Importance, to me, creates the energy of urgency. You should prioritize those things of importance and give them urgency instead of allowing urgent things to become important. The importance is created by the actuality of the situation or event and not the urgency perceived by others. I have made huge business mistakes because I'll be in the middle of something important and my wife will call me with something "urgent", such as we've run out of milk and she needs for me to pick some up on the way home. I am not saying that getting milk on the way home is not important, but the level of that importance needs to be prioritized, especially when it comes to time. I've now lost clarity, balance, and focus on the matter that was more important. Had my child been starving and my wife was completely unable to feed my child, now we have an urgent situation

> "You don't need to outdo the competition. It's expensive and defensive. Underdo your competition. We need more simplicity and clarity."
>
> Jason Fried

that is also very important. Obviously, everything needs to be put into context and we need to create urgency by the importance of the situation.

A good portion of the time, this urgency is created by emotion combined with a lack of focus and balance. I used to play defensive back on my college football team and I would live and die by each play. This is an extremely dangerous way to play that particular position because the best way to be a defensive back is to have a very short-term memory. Instead of me being an emotional wreck on the field, my coach taught me to "just keep playing" because each new play is just another opportunity. This created a "majesty of calmness" and balance so that I could take each play as it came. By not making every play "urgent" – that certain plays were more important than others – I became a much better defensive back.

Throughout the day, we are all faced with many distractions, be it in life or in business. And how many times have we lost track of focus because of something urgent, not important, and then forgotten to do the important thing? The point is that we all need to just "keep playing", but stick to our important plan. So although my wife may need me to pick up milk on the way home, I have constant reminders around me at the office that this is not more important at this time than doing what is next on, say, my action item list or vision board.

Something I have found important is that before I take action, I pause a few seconds to meditate or shift my energy so that I have clarity to create velocity. In business, before I make a sales call, I meditate for 5 or 10 seconds. I shut my eyes and get in touch with my senses. I see, feel, hear and believe that I will have no resistance, take a deep breath and say, "I will receive no resistance" before I pick up the phone. People at Sports 1 Marketing will confirm that this works. I've had employees come in and tell me that, despite their best efforts, they've been unable to reach someone for weeks. I'll pick up the

> "Clarity, clarity, surely clarity is the Most beautiful thing in the world, A limited, limiting clarity I have not and never did have any Motive of poetry But to achieve clarity."
>
> George Oppen

phone and get the person on my first attempt. This is the energy that I put out there. Talk in terms of solutions, not problems. If you get frustrated, have resistance, or create negative intentions or energy then this is the kind of energy you will attract in return. What you resist … persists!

Let me explain the meaning of the expression "What you resist persists", first by way of examples. Consider those parents who, instead of teaching their children about what they'll find out there in the world and empowering their children to make value-based decisions, they resist and tell their children exactly what they must do. The children who couldn't watch television become obsessed with it. The kids who couldn't have dessert inevitably become overweight as adults. The parents manifest these things into their lives. What you resist persists.

What you resist persists. It is so fundamentally true that it bears repeating. When I was working for Leigh, I used to commute from

Rancho Santa Fe to Newport Beach, a 75 mile trip that would take no less than an hour and half each way. Every day at 4:30 PM, I'd start worrying that Leigh might have something else for me to do so that I couldn't go home and have family time with my wife and kids. And every time I'd think this, sure enough, Leigh would call me in to his office and I wouldn't leave for home until 7:00 PM. And the whole way home, among other things, I'd be thinking that my wife was going to kill me and I was going to miss the kids before they went to bed. And, yes, every single time I got exactly what I manifested or was trying to resist! Then I started connecting to source and saying to myself, "I will have no resistance leaving the office, I will have no resistance with traffic getting home…" And on those few occasions I did run late, I'd say to myself, "I have an understanding wife who'll just be glad I am home safely, and I'll still be able to put my children to bed." And this is exactly what happened.

Our ego tells us that if we control our own destiny, then we must be able to control all of those things in order to achieve our vision. This puts velocity through an unstable foundation because it is better to be a good bet of the universe than it is to just bet on yourself. If the vision has negative energy then "Cancel!" it and get clear and meditate on what it is you really desire or want to achieve.

How important is it to "Cancel" negative thoughts? We have 12,000 to 50,000 thoughts in a day, and our mind takes the negative

> "Thoughts lead on to purposes; purposes go forth in action; actions form habits; habits decide character; and character fixes our destiny."
>
> Tyron Edwards

approach to things 70% of the time. Globally speaking, since we must use our free will to connect to source or goodness, your mind, naturally, thinks about what you don't have, what you can't do. Not to get too scientific and I am in no way a biology expert, but I learned that the amygdala in the brain modulates the release of cortisol and other stress hormones, creating anxiety and fear. Anxiety is created by the unknown and other future-based factors, and is the usual cause of the cortisol release. Like a high-octane drink, cortisol gives us the energy jolt needed to overcome an emergency, but everything in life seemingly has become an emergency. Our brains now keep us on DEFCOM 5 alert with constant cortisol production resulting in serious health problems like high blood pressure and glucose levels. Even more damaging is the negative energy it attracts. Common sense tells us that chain drinking high-octane beverages will prove to be detrimental to our health. Similarly, we need to tell our brains

> "The beauty is that through disappointment you can gain clarity, and with clarity comes conviction and true originality."
>
> Conan O'Brien

to stop producing excessive levels of cortisol and start producing serotonin, which does all kinds of wonderful things for creativity, happiness and health. This is the scientific reason why we need to turn our thoughts around and make them positive and clear. This will reduce your anxiety and keep you open to learning.

Turning to a business example, this is why, for instance, if I get resistance on a business call, I am the only one accountable for it. I say this because I must trust the universe and use my free will to connect with source. Anything that I am attracting into my life is based on the energy that I am putting out there. But I know that I'm human and, therefore, I'm not 100% aligned or connected all the time with source or goodness. So if I do run into a challenging or resisting prospect, I need to look within myself to see what I'm doing to attract such energy. The more I reflect, however, the more statistically successful I become and the less resistance I end up facing. Because I've now done this long enough and proven this to myself, I trust the universe even more. In fact, in trusting the universe, I've found that those who have appeared to be challenging, skeptical or resisting prospects initially have statistically been the ones who've proved the easiest to reengineer and share a vision with later. I have utilized my energy to shift their energy and change their initial resistance. Now, a challenging, skeptical or resisting prospect is akin to a tough negotiator. These are people who I will willingly do business with and are very different from the "dick" referenced by Leigh. Someone is not a "dick" just because they might not share my vision. I consider a "dick" to be someone who is not connected to source or goodness and brings such a dishonest, destructive negative energy to the table that, on a gut level, I can sense. I instinctively know that these are the people who I won't do business with.

So, you, yourself, stay connected to goodness and keep the connection clean. Again, the universe is eternally abundant. It has no "Empty". There is enough of everything for everyone.

GUIDEPOST PRINCIPLE – KEY ELEMENT #2: BALANCE

Balance is an equipoised state that, with clarity, takes into consideration all of the different values that you have. Balance creates stability that allows you to maximize the velocity created by the Key Element of Clarity!

The need for balance is far from a new concept. Aristotle's primary philosophy stressed that a balanced life leads to a happy life and we should all strive for a "Golden Mean". The

> "What I dream of is an art of balance."
>
> Henri Matisse

"Golden Mean" is not a strictly delineated middle point between two extremes, but varies depending upon the situation. To him, it would have been just as important to have ice cream as to make sure you had something from each of the four food groups. He would have found it equally important not to overeat as it would be not to under eat. He would have found it important to balance our time with our family, friends and work.

But while the need for balance is pivotal to all of the Key Elements and Principles in this book, it is not as complex as it sounds. To keep balanced, we just need to be connected to source or goodness. If we are connected, the balance itself will become more apparent as we'll attract those things that keep us balanced. By trusting the universe, if we need to spend more time with our family, it will come to us. Similarly, if we need to spend more time working, this will come to us as well.

But, what if you have velocity without balance and, therefore, no stability? Many who have tremendous velocity, tremendous energy, such as the great openers in business, lack stability, and this creates potentially huge problems. This is true both physically and spiritually. Picture a car going 200 miles per hour down a highway losing a wheel. The end result is an evitable crash. A Ferrari can't even approach 20 miles per hour if it has a flat tire.

I thought I had great ideas when I was young. I knew that I also had great energy and free will (determination), and I was willing to work very hard for the things that I wanted very badly. I thought this was all that I needed. I didn't understand how everything was interconnected and how important it was, for example, to be more interested than interesting.

> "Fortunate indeed, is the man who takes exactly the right measure of himself, and holds a just balance between what he can acquire and what he can use."
>
> Peter Mere Latham

When I was in my twenties I started one of the first online gambling sites. Without thinking how it was interconnected to so many negative energies, I expended a lot of time, money and energy only to find out that even the best case scenario meant having to leave the U.S. because I could not collect the revenue legally. In the end, it may have been a great idea on its surface, but with more due diligence and experience, I could have avoided the "dummy tax".

Everything in the universe vibrates, and in order to maximize the energy within the vibration, you need clarity. When you have clarity, it creates velocity. When you are clear on a specific objective, you vibrate faster or create speed. But in order to utilize the speed, you need to have stability or balance. Remember, the earth and its minerals vibrate the slowest, followed by plants, which vibrate slower than animals with humans vibrating faster. Most importantly, human mental waves vibrate the fastest and will attract with great speed and accuracy.

Consider the typical teenager who wants a car. This will be all they think about. They'll even go to the dealership to sit in the car to see how it feels and smells. Regardless of their financial situation, they'll somehow end up manifesting that car for themselves. For me, it was the golf course I discussed in Section 1; from walking courses, to taking pictures, to reading magazines, I did everything I could to mentally attract owning a golf course. Once again, I learned many valuable lessons and wish I would have evaluated owning a golf course in Virginia with the Balance of all my Foundation Values. I did learn one incredible lesson about owning a golf course, though. Always be the third owner!

> "Action is at bottom a swinging and flailing of the arms to regain one's balance and keep afloat."
>
> Eric Hoffer

GUIDEPOST PRINCIPLE – KEY ELEMENT #3: FOCUS

What sense would it make to have a six-foot foundation if you want to construct a hotel on it? Similarly, why would you want to build a circular dome on a rectangular foundation? We want to take the Balance and Clarity Key Elements that we have and align them with what we want to manifest. We do this by way of *focus* which creates accuracy. We want to manifest what we desire as fast and accurately as we can.

We need to be precise with our directed attention, but that doesn't necessarily mean that you can't think globally and still be focused. Say you want to manifest world peace. If you focused on world peace and we could motivate everyone else to manifest world peace as well, we'd have world peace. Again, when we focus individually on what we want and can take it to the next level by empowering others to manifest the same thing, that energy now becomes collective and can manifest global intentions. For any doubters, look to Fairfield, IA where everyone collectively meditates and manifests twice a day. Beyond the subjective peace and tranquility a visitor will find in visiting Fairfield, resultant objective standards exist as well. Fairfield is one of the safest cities in the U.S. with crime dropping by 35% since 1999 and continuing to drop every year.

> "The key to realizing a dream is to focus not on success but significance – and then even the small steps and little victories along your path will take on greater meaning."
>
> Oprah Winfrey

Usually, when someone works hard, but does not accomplish their goal, accuracy is a major problem. They did not take all the necessary steps to succeed. How important is accuracy? If you have a stable, fast rocket to take you to the moon, but are off in your calculations, you'll never make your destination. You need to be precise. Otherwise, you'll be like the person who wanted to manifest a lot of dough and ended up with his Aunt Susie at his door with a plate of cookies instead of money.

This doesn't mean that your approach to achieve your precise manifestation is always direct. Leigh Steinberg, for instance, has a tactic he called, "Spheres of Influence". The concept is to approach people you know to ultimately get to share a vision or "align" with another person without going directly to that other person. Leigh used this concept to approach football recruits. Because so many people were pursuing these top prospects, the recruits had their guards up and Leigh realized that he could not afford to be obsequious. He recognized the need to be strategic in utilizing the "Spheres of Influence" so that the idea of Leigh representing them became the recruit's, and they'd either let their guard down or even start pursing him rather than vice versa.

The "Spheres of Influence" are equally applicable to life and business. Although I'm using a football recruiting example, the idea is to reach the person in the bull's-eye of the diagram by approaching those in the outer rings, with each consecutively smaller ring representing a closer connection to that individual, *even* if you personally know that central individual. This obviously is aligned with everything and everyone being connected. You want to convince those

> "You cannot depend on your eyes when your imagination is out of focus."
> Mark Twain

around your central figure first and motivate or stimulate them to align with what you want them to do; you want to share a vision with these people so that they then, in turn, will take action on your behalf, ultimately leading to your central figure, who will then reach out to you.

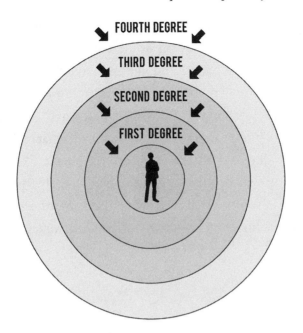

Naturally, you have strategic reasons for approaching these other people in the first place, in the same way you would approach someone to make an introduction on your behalf; you would certainly not approach anyone irrelevant to or ill-thought by the person in the middle, who you ultimately want to influence. But even if you personally know the central figure, your credibility is enhanced by the use of these "influential" assets, and by an indirect rather than a direct involvement. After all, isn't it

> "A mind troubled by doubt cannot focus on the course to victory."
>
> Arthur Golden

better to have someone else, who is influential, singing your praise than to brag about yourself? Think the first degree of Kevin Bacon's Six Degrees of Separation, except the more masterful you get, the greater the degrees away you can be and still be effective. In fact, using the right psychologies and motivating factors, you might find it even more influential if you could talk to a Fourth Separated, who you know would tell the Third Separated, who is directly related to a

Second Separated, who is an in-law to the First Separated, the subject's best friend. This is because you now have something that appears complete, original, unbiased and authentic content despite the fact that it is 100% biased and orchestrated. The truth is the information was completely systematically, strategically and psychologically manifested. It's like a game of chess crossed with that credible person you ask to make the introduction on your behalf exponentially employed. Since there are many strategies available to achieve an objective, it is essential that we stay focused in order to utilize our velocity with accuracy to rapidly manifest what we truly desire!

GUIDEPOST PRINCIPLE – KEY ELEMENT #4: CONFIDENCE

Clarity/velocity, balance/stability and focus/accuracy lead to the ability to attract what we desire with confidence, and that attraction occurs more rapidly. This applies to every part of life as well as business. Confidence is important because it is a positive energy that is connected to source or goodness, and emitting it to others will result in others emitting it back to you. They will trust you and they will like you, which are two critical components of sharing a vision with someone. After all, as the old Hasidic saying goes, "The man who has confidence in himself gains the confidence of others."

> "You have to have confidence in your ability, and then be tough enough to follow through."
> Rosalynn Carter

Remember, though, that the universe is subject to the laws of physics, and, as vibrating cells full of energy, electricity and conductivity, we need to be aware of what we are attracting because we are capable of attracting whatever it is we want as well as what we don't want to attract into our lives. In a cosmic, spiritual, high-level and global sense, like attracts like. That is how we manifest things. Because I put the strongest power and energy out there, it either attracts whatever it is that I don't have enough of, or exactly what it is I want. I find it difficult to separate the connection to source and goodness from business and life because of the laws of the universe; wherever I go, I should be attracting what I want in my life, which is to make a lot of money, help a lot of people, and have a lot of fun. But the choice is each of ours. With whatever it is you want to attract, you are the one common denominator in your life, and accountable for everything and everyone in it ... which is why it is so important to maintain a connection to goodness.

But, because like attracts like, as advised, be careful, especially in business. For example, if you oversell someone, someone will oversell you. If you backend sell someone, someone will backend sell you. I promise you that if you cheat someone, it will happen back. When I retired at the age of thirty-eight, I felt, at times, that I had cheated the system. I felt too much had come too easily at too young of an age and I didn't deserve it. These were the energies I was putting out there at that time. I eventually came to realize what it was that I really wanted to attract. I, like almost every other "too small to be a pro" athlete, wanted to be a sports agent. Later, after manifesting my partnership with Leigh Steinberg, I wanted to be Warren Moon's partner. This is where I focused my energy and this is what I attracted.

> "Self-confidence is the first requisite to great undertakings."
> Samuel Johnson

It is important to remember, what you think, speak or do will come back to you. What you do to others will come back to you. It is physically impossible to attract something different than what you're exerting. If you are a decent person, people will be decent to you. No truer words were spoken than "The more you give, the more you will get back." Who you are will attract people like you to you. What you don't like in others is what you don't like in yourself. What aggravates you about others is what aggravates you about yourself. You will be amazed what can happen for you by simply understanding this. It's the cause and effect of karma, what we give out is what we receive, including our projections. So, again, if we project our insecurities, sure enough, we will attract back more people with that insecurity. For instance, if I don't like backstabbers and people talking behind my back and I said, "I can't believe that person said something behind my back," all I will accomplish is having more people stab me in, and talk behind, my back because this is something I don't like about myself that I am projecting … and yet I'm doing it.

This is not to say that I don't find myself saying the word "Cancel" to myself to negate my own negative inner chatter at times in order not to draw a "like" negative energy; I don't want that thought out there in the universe. It would be like the old Russian Bubbes sitting along the beach on a summer vacation in Siberia complaining, "Oy, if only it were cooler."

See what happened! Once you understand this concept, you'll never look back. In my opinion, it is a form of enlightenment. Your

> "Attempt easy tasks as if they were difficult, and difficult as if they were easy; in the one case that confidence may not fall asleep, in the other that it may not be dismayed."
>
> Baltasar Gracian

entire world will expand. It will be part of you forever.

How does time fit into this idea of attraction? Nothing is more frustrating and confusing in understanding how the universe works than trying to understand the variable of time. Nothing is more confusing than quantum and metaphysics and grasping with the notion that what is happening now may have already happened and will happen in the future, or a consideration of what plane we are all on. You need not worry about the variable of time. As always, you need only to trust the universe. Get out of your own way and realize that if you are clear, balanced and focused and have put velocity, stability and accuracy in play, you will attract what you desire and have manifested. It will come to you. You need not be Sisyphus forever struggling to push that boulder up the mountain only to watch it roll back down. I venture to guess that 90% of the people out there struggle with that "boulder" in their cubicles on a daily basis, and wonder why they never get over the hump. You need not climb to the top of the highest mountain to get the gold ring. You can sit at the bottom of the mountain and attract the gold ring down onto your finger.

People often try to put an expectation of time onto their manifestations. They also frequently attempt to put an expectation of time onto karma and the laws of attraction. Unfortunately, the universe does not work that way within our means and realms; otherwise, we'd be vibrating so fast that we'd be enlightened to the full picture and

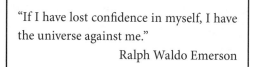

"If I have lost confidence in myself, I have the universe against me."

Ralph Waldo Emerson

specificity of our desired intentions and no longer have a need to be here. How fulfilling would it be to exist with everything and everyone in our life exactly as we desire! There would be world peace, we could win the lottery at will, have the perfect wife and kids, and most importantly, the San Diego Chargers would win the Super Bowl every year! I know, at first glance, this sounds attractive, but as we know, the journey is really the fulfilling part, the learning process coming from recognizing our mistakes and making the adjustments needed to move forward. Always being right would quickly get boring – to the point where we'd never have a reason to get out of bed in the morning because we could no longer be surprised. If we can control our perception of time and the patience that comes with it, as well as trust the universe, then we'll be able to manifest things more rapidly for that very reason – it or they will manifest themselves at the time that is appropriate for that particular manifestation or manifestations.

As an example, have you ever wished you were there already when you're driving, especially when you're running late? Don't things seem to take so much longer? I don't know about you, but I find a stop light seems to last so much longer when I'm running late. Of course, in actuality, the cycle for that traffic light hasn't changed. So, if you can learn to remove time as an expectation variable from the equation and stop rushing things, you can then focus more clearly, become more accurate, and have greater stability toward obtaining your goal.

You will actually achieve your goal faster than if you keep getting in your own way, constantly thinking, "Why is this taking so long?" Quite simply, things take the amount of time they are supposed to take. As Maria Robinson wrote, "There's no need to rush. If something is meant to be, it will happen – in the right time, with the right person, and for the best reason." When you're ready, it will come, and it will come more accurately and rapidly if you stay connected to goodness.

> "Education is the ability to listen to almost anything without losing your temper or your self-confidence."
>
> Robert Frost

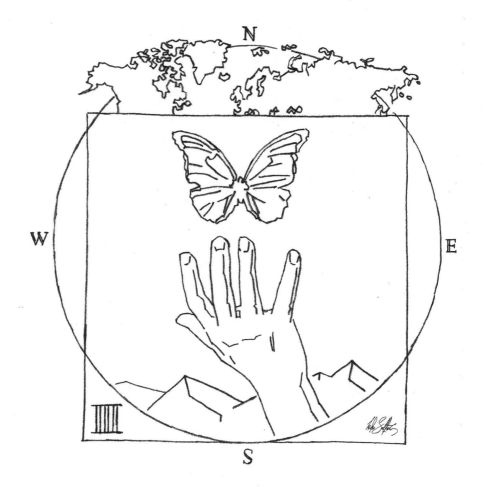

III. PRINCIPAL THREE: MANIFESTATION

> "Every great work, every great accomplishment, has been brought into manifestation through holding to the vision, and often just before the big achievement, comes apparent failure and discouragement."

> Florence Scovel Shinn

In order to manifest what we desire we must align with and trust the universe, focusing our energy to connect to source first, then having the execution and manifestation of our desires. This is where 80% of our energy needs to be spent. Most people are great starters or openers. They spend the majority of their energy and focus on how to stimulate interest or share a vision. They do not understand that this is only 20% of the journey. The true energy that thrives is the energy after you come to an agreement or a promise (or staying connected to source). To create and manifest our desires personally and even beyond, globally, we must be "ordinary" + "extra", or in other words, "extraordinary" and exceed expectations and create energy that creates its own energy. Then we can manifest what we desire faster and more accurately. Remember: "The extra mile is never crowded."

Manifestation Principle – Key Element #1: Perspective

Perspective is Everything! Appreciation is the DNA for your perspective. Let's first look at the definition of appreciation. The word "appreciate" means to add value. Therefore, whenever and whatever we appreciate we add value to. It's important to appreciate everything all the time.

Poppa, my grandfather, was 95 when my grandmother passed away, and I took him from the house they had lived in forever

> "You must look within for value, but must look beyond for perspective."
>
> Denis Waitley

to a nursing home. You'd think he'd be terrified, right? He'd just lost his wife after 67 years of marriage and was moving into a new environment with a host of strangers.

Well, upon entering the lobby of the nursing home, he declared immediately, "I love my room!"

Yes, his eyesight was bad, but he was still sharp. So it came as no surprise when I said, "Poppa, this isn't your room," and he replied, "I know that, fool. I love it though."

"But you've haven't seen it," I gently corrected him.

"I can't see it," he responded, then added, "but I only have one choice, right?"

The way he said it was neither in bitterness nor despair, but in great appreciation, and you could feel the positive energy. With my clear vision and positive outlook, I always thought myself a Toptomist, the top of all optimists, and here I was supplanted by a Poptomist, a man with even greater experience, appreciation and value added to his existence than me!

Another great example is what I have taught thousands of people around the world. The easiest way to change your life is simply saying "Thank you." You cannot over say these two words. They are amazing on so many different levels in so many different philosophies and religions, and so easy to say. It is so vital to be sure to say it to everyone, but if all you did was say "Thank you" before you went to bed and when you woke up in the morning – two words, twice a day – I promise you that your life would change. The words create positive momentum, and people love positive reinforcement for doing something. They create a perceived appreciation, and I cannot state it enough that appreciation adds value. And if it adds value, it adds energy; it is a direct connection to source and goodness.

> "People often say that 'beauty is in the eye of the beholder,' and I say that the most liberating thing about beauty is realizing that you are the beholder. This empowers us to find beauty in places where others have not dared to look, including inside ourselves."
>
> Salma Hayek

So appreciate everything and everyone. Instead of taking offense to a scathing phone call or email, make it a point to appreciate the situation; appreciate that, perhaps, the other person is having a hard time. Attempt to add value to people who you touch, or to a room upon entering by making it a better place.

I submit: whether you think you can or you can't do something, either way, you will be right. This is because you are the only common denominator in any life, especially in your business. Yet, if we utilize the 80/20/80 Rule when analyzing Accountability, only 20% of the population lives above the line in accountability. Only 20% of the population take responsibility and recognize that they are the only ones that connect to source and goodness for themselves, while 80% live their life below the line in blame, shame and justification.

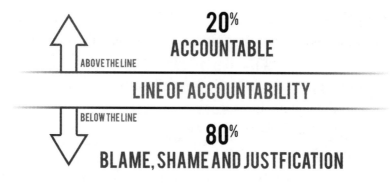

You can blame whomever you want or be shamed for your circumstances, or you can try to justify what happened … or you can take charge and manifest for yourself. As Maria Robinson wrote:

> "The extent to which you can achieve your dreams depends on the extent to which you take responsibility for your life. When you blame others for what you're going through, you deny responsibility – you give others power over that part of your life."

I will use my clarity, balance, and focus to create velocity through my value-based foundation to accurately attract what I wish to manifest and be completely accountable for it! I just need to keep my awareness and perspective positive by connecting to source or goodness, by appreciating everyone and everything!

> "I believe everyone should have a broad picture of how the universe operates and our place in it. It is a basic human desire. And it also puts our worries in perspective."
>
> Stephen Hawking

In order to utilize all of your senses you need to be aware. There are no accidents. Watch what is happening around you. Be aware of those people and things that you are attracting into your life, especially the ones that are being attracted repetitively. If you are more interested than interesting, you will be more aware. For example, a few weeks ago, I kept seeing lizards in my backyard and parking lot at the office. Being more interested than interesting, I looked up the symbolic meanings of "Lizards" and found it to be directly aligned with a personal challenge I was facing. With the arrival of my son, our house became a little too small, but I kept going round and round on the decision of whether to look for a new house or not. Because of their ability to lose then regrow their tails, lizards symbolically stand for the concept of "letting go" of something troubling you and moving on. Being aware of little signs like these can prove to be very significant in our lives.

Even with great awareness are you going to succeed at everything you do? I hope not ... the journey is the success. There is no way to happiness. Happiness is the way. It's all about perspective. Just ask Poppa.

Manifestation Principle – Key Element #2: Free Will

Being a go-getter with a great power of intention and energy, I could not understand when I was younger why, as Teddy Roosevelt stressed, people just didn't work hard in order to succeed. Meditation, "get out of your own way", and the like had no meaning to me because I could create

> "Life is like a game of cards. The hand that is dealt you is determinism; the way you play it is free will."
>
> Jawaharlal Nehru

unbelievable velocity. And then, as I got my own clarity, I realized that Teddy Roosevelt was only partially right. It was not so much the "free will" of intention to work really hard to overcome obstacles as it was the "free will" to focus on connecting to source and goodness. If I did the latter, there would be no obstacles. If I utilized my "free will" in every situation to connect to source, then I realized that everything I desired – because the universe only knows the word "Yes" and is abundant – would happen faster and more accurately. I would empower myself to be the person I wanted to be. I could also make decisions more efficiently and effectively to manifest or execute on whatever my objective was.

But beware. There is one thing that can interfere with, corrode, or disconnect this "free will" connection to source or goodness – our ego!

Our ego tells us what we think we need, which acts as a block or obstacle to source or goodness. Egos cause us to get in our own way and waste energy, instead of us trusting the universe to manifest our dreams. You need to really explore the purported needs dictated by your ego because you will find that you do not need any of them, and the more quickly you reach this realization, the less negative energy you will have wasted and the more positive energy you will have to manifest your dream.

What are some of these needs which act as obstacles to our ability to connect? Well, we have a need to feel offended. This occurs when we are not connected to goodness and lack confidence. If someone says, "I don't like the way your hair looks," you will only be offended if you don't believe "I like the way I look." You cannot be defined by what someone else says or thinks about you; they do not have that power. They do have the power to define themselves as someone who is not connected or nice. For example, how can I be offended if someone thinks I have a big nose, while the fact of the matter is that I have a small face? In all seriousness, if you don't worry about what others think, this need vanishes. You are not what others think of you!

> "It is well to be up before daybreak, for such habits contribute to health, wealth, and wisdom."
>
> Aristotle

One of the other ways that I used to be offended was when I felt left out. This happens to many people. Why wasn't I invited or included? Divest yourself of the need to bring energy to things like this. For example, what if your friend only had one extra ticket and wanted to include you, but his mother insisted he take his brother? Should we be offended?

Another ego-based need is to be superior or win at all costs. Why? Instead, just desire to be the best that we can be and connect to goodness. When our free will connects to source and goodness then everyone wins (or the one who can keep their connection non-corroded will always win). You will be happier when you realize that life really isn't a competition. There's plenty of everything for everyone. When you trust the universe and realize that the universe is infinitely abundant, you will be able to attract whatever it is you want to attract. The only scarcity in the universe is the resolve, the effective habits, the discipline, and the energy to go and get it ... and the gratitude or appreciation that goes with it.

Our ego can have us thinking that we're better than someone else. Focus instead on being a better person, a better self, a better you. Have as your objective that every place you enter and every person you meet feels better for having met you. In other words, appreciate everything and everyone, and you will add value to it!

Our ego also tells us that we have a need to be right. How many arguments have taken place, moreover how many wars have been fought over this need? I think there are many occasions when you can allow someone to be right even when

> "Habit is necessary; it is the habit of having habits, of turning a trail into a rut, that must be incessantly fought against if one is to remain alive."
>
> Edith Wharton

you believe they're not, or, at least, agree to disagree. Anyone in, or who has been in a relationship knows this need very well. My adorable wife goes so far as to do the "I told you so dance" whenever I make an ass out of myself trying to argue for the certainty of something that doesn't exist. She raises her hand and dances around me singing "I told you so, I told you so," just to remind me who is always right. More importantly, though, there is no need to be right.

Most egos also create a need to have more. Remember "more" is too general. It actually carries a disconnected energy of scarcity. If you want more, this assumes that there is less or not enough. If you focus your energy on not having enough, that is exactly what the universe will bring to you. Remember: the universe is abundant, and there is enough of everything for everyone. Also, remember that the universe is precise, so be specific as to what you desire to manifest it. Be careful to manifest specifically what you want and not let your ego demand more just to have more! For example, a common desire many people have is to find a partner or spouse in life. Many people obsess on one true love for them in the universe or Ms./Mr. Right.

Instead of focusing on the specifics of what they are looking for, they carry a scarce energy that they can't find Mr. Right. Instead of focusing on the lack of Mr. Right, they should focus in on a short 5'7", brown hair, brown-eyed, dark and handsome man who is financially secure and funny…basically someone like me! Maybe that would be a need for too much!

Our ego's need for more appears to be the most common need in America, but not necessarily in the world. Indeed, philosophies, health theories, and even business

> "All the world is birthday cake, so take a piece, but not too much."
> George Harrison

principles exist that adhere to the belief that "more is less". So, we can't need to have more all of the time. It's a bad trait to carry. Instead of wasting energy, allow the universe to be abundant, which means the universe will provide everybody with exactly what they desire. The difference is subtle, but huge. If you believe you want different or specific things, this is not the same as believing you want or need more. If you believe that you can manifest different things to create greater fulfillment, additional positive energy and a more valuable purpose in the context of the totality of the Principles in this book, this is not the same thing as just wanting *more*.

A classic example of the need to want more is when Americans buy sodas the size of gas barrels. Why do we need so much soda? It is our ego that drives us to super-size everything even though no 16-year-old alive can finish a 64 ounce super soda and a bucket of popcorn the size of a wash tub. There is no scarcity in the universe. We can continue to make more popcorn and soda to satisfy everybody!

Another need that our egos center around is the need for accolades or awards. It's hard to fathom in our society today that we do not need to achieve awards or accolades. We need to trust the universe that we are going to put the positive thoughts and energy out there and it will attract what we desire. And whatever that existence is, others may perceive or define it as some sort of achievement and give us accolades or awards, yet the action or energy speaks for itself. If we work hard to connect to source and manifest the outcomes we desire, others may want to recognize these manifestations with awards. But be advised, many people may become jealous and project negative energy toward us. We must know that our connections to source and these external perceptions of us have no effect on or for us, nor do they have the right to define us unless we allow them to exist.

> "If you spend all your time worrying about what others think, you will eventually forget how to think for yourself."
>
> Nishan Panwar

For example, Warren Moon, my partner, has won almost every award in football from the MVP of the Rose Bowl to the NFL Man of the Year. But all of these awards sit safely in a storage facility because Warren's ego and enlightenment has evolved to a point that his only concern is that he stays connected to goodness. One of Warren's ultimate desires is to change the attitudes toward African Americans in the world. This vision far exceeds any trophy or plaque that has been bestowed on him. Similarly, he gives no energy to all of those haters in Michigan who are still bitter over Warren's exceptional performance that led to the Washington Huskies' upset over them in the Rose Bowl. Warren stays connected to source and goodness so he attracts people who are like him, and not the ones who admire him for his awards or accolades.

Finally, regarding ego, you do not need to put energy into or focus on your reputation, good or bad. You are never as good as they say you are, or ever as bad. How much energy is wasted worrying about what other people think of you? Worry is a wasted emotion, and we need to be connected, confident, and shifting our energy when we get worried. Our families, for instance, often think too highly of us and this is where entitlement comes from. Beyond our family, though, some people are haters. They look for scarcity and lack and revel in other people's misery. They find comfort in, what I can only describe as, these competitive outward looking relationships. But the only person we need to worry about is ourselves. There is only one person who knows every single thing about you, and that is you. You and only you are the person who you need to depend on the most. Yes, be aware of what other people say, positive

> "The forces of good and evil are working within and around me, I must choose, and in a free will universe I do have a choice."
>
> Sovereign

and negative, but at its core, your focus needs to be on what you believe, and what you can manifest, and using your free will to connect to and staying connected to source and goodness.

If you have the right perspective and you are making good use of your free will by doing your best to stay connected to goodness or source, you now need to step out of your personal vacuum and make sure you're on the right page with others. This is how manifestation ultimately occurs … for you, for others and then, as will be discussed, beyond.

> "Successful diplomacy is an alignment of objectives and means."
>
> Dennis Ross

If you recall, the AAA Strategy starts with Alignment then proceeds on to Action and Adjustment. Alignment is where you spend your time being more interested than interesting by planning and thinking. Action is where you actually implement the plan under discussion. Finally, you need to prepare for Adjustment; despite the fact that we would like to be omniscient beings (as I believed I was when I was in my twenties), we are not; so be ready to put aside your ego and needs, and understand that we must continually change and evolve.

Alignment, however, is the first step and is crucial for everything else to fall into place in order to maintain our connection to source and manifest what we desire more accurately and rapidly. In life, we must constantly align with our partners, our children, our friends; as well as with weekend plans, opportunities, day care pickups … the list goes on and on. When negotiating, we must align the variables of time, emotion, and value; and recognize when they are out of alignment. Therefore, you want to spend 80% of your focus and time on alignment. You constantly need to ask questions, being more interested than interesting, making sure you fully

> "Action is a great restorer and builder of confidence. Inaction is not only the result, but the cause, of fear. Perhaps the action you take will be successful; perhaps different action or adjustments will have to follow. But any action is better than no action at all."
>
> Norman Vincent Peale

understand the reasons, impacts, and capabilities of the situation. As will be discussed later, you'll ask open-ended or non-leading questions to get people to describe what their intentions are. You'll follow with closed-ended or leading questions to align with what they want and what you want to help them with, and to ensure that you are discussing the same data, reaching the same goals, doing things the same way.

Repeating or summarizing what someone says is a good way to double check on whether or not you have alignment. When I conclude with "Does that sound fair?" or "Is there any reason we shouldn't move forward?", I am actually providing a summary statement that what I proposed to you is aligned with your values that you have articulated. Of course, this makes sense at the conclusion of a business meeting in order to know what everyone's agreed on and what happens next, but this is also a great device for making sure you are aligned with virtually anyone about virtually anything.

For example, one of my valuable employees forgot to follow one of my subtleties of success and failed to immediately calendar a re-scheduling of an important canceled phone conference. Of course, this resulted in him neglecting to do it later, and had I not happened to inquire about this particular matter, I would've been out of town and missed conferencing in from afar. After I went through and provided him with constructive criticism to ensure that he wouldn't repeat this mistake, I ended with, "Does that sound fair?" I used a mechanism of alignment where he had to agree and say "Yes." This indicated to me that he would do his best to immediately place things into the calendar when changes occurred.

I've provided you with direct instances of alignment, but you can make sure you have alignment by copying people on emails, reviewing invoices, tracking and agreeing to changes on documents as well as a host of other ways. Personally, I prefer the direct method when at all possible because there is less room for error. Alignment ultimately leads to a fulfillment in the relationship and a shared vision between parties. Managing and developing that shared vision with action and adjustment will lead to manifestation and success. If, however, you exceed that shared vision – those clearly envisioned and defined objectives or expectations – your manifestation and success will grow to the "nth" Power.

> "If you're trying to achieve, there will be roadblocks. I've had them; everybody has had them. But obstacles don't have to stop you. If you run into a wall, don't turn around and give up. Figure out how to climb it, go through it, or work around it."
> Michael Jordan

MANIFESTATION PRINCIPLE - KEY ELEMENT #4: THE "NTH" POWER

Mathematically speaking, the "nth" Power exponentially takes a number from its base and continues to multiply itself by itself stopping only when it reaches "n", which can be indefinitely defined. In the utopic state of "thrivation", we are creating and taking energy to that indefinite "nth" Power. The energy has grown exponentially and has scaled itself.

Anyone who is a parent understands this concept. At its simplest level, you and someone else, two vibrating balls of energy, have co-manifested and propagated a new energy form, who will, hopefully, become your empowered legacy that you fill with your thoughts, energy and love that they, in turn, can give to other people. And the energy created keeps recreating and scaling itself and continues on through eternity – to the "nth" Power.

As another example, I put knowledge or mental waves out there as my energy to you. You then take the knowledge that I've imparted and teach it to ten people. These ten people then teach it to ten more people apiece. Now you have 100 people who go off to teach. Through this example, you can see the re-creation, scaling and continuation of this energy occurring. This is exactly how creating a collective belief or collective energy can have a global affect! In my case, I would like to empower as many people as I can to connect to source or goodness. In broad terms, energy creates everything you want on its own, but you need to put in all of the work, all of the Principles and Key Elements. We want things to thrive because it makes things easier, it multiplies exponentially and scales. When something thrives that you

> "A man can scale almost anything for which he has unlimited enthusiasm."
> Charles M. Schwab

initiated with your energy, those things you put energy into carry the same energy you do. For instance, in business when we want to sell,

95

we first need to stimulate interest or put energy into the universe to connect to source. But as our business progresses, we continually use our free will to connect to source so we can then transition that interest or energy, share a vision, then stay connected to goodness to manage that vision and exceed expectations so that things will thrive. Now instead of having to sell to separate individuals one at a time, if you can manage and exceed expectations, you actually increase your statistical success by selling more efficiently.

Apple is an excellent example of a thriving company. Customers pleased with products they directly purchased from Apple create additional sales for Apple simply by talking to others about their purchased products because Apple and its products have exceeded their expectations. So, not only will a happy Apple customer continue to buy Apple products, but an Apple customer sitting in first class who praises their MacBook when questioned by the PC user sitting next to him or her creates many more sales for Apple. Personally, I thought myself a lifetime PC and Blackberry user until my Executive Vice President Scott Carter changed my perspective. Like others, he has helped take Apple to the "nth" Power as I have spent thousands of dollars on Apple products both personal and for our business ever since, yet they have never had to spend a dime to directly sell me a thing!

Just as Apple has thrived to the "nth" Power and become one of the most successful companies in the world, you too can thrive to the "nth" Power and manifest what you desire more rapidly and accurately individually. But, most importantly, you can inspire and empower others to manifest collectively with you and thrive to the "nth" Power!

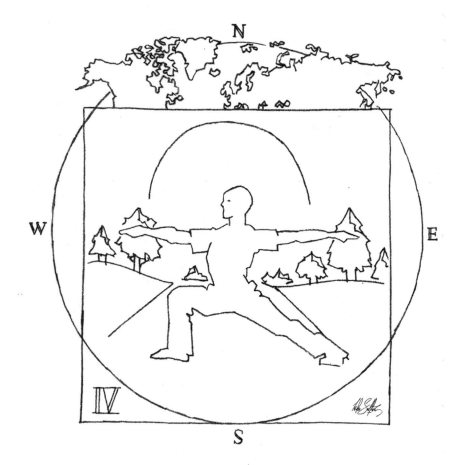

IV. PRINCIPLE FOUR: DISCIPLINE

"Discipline is the bridge between goals
and accomplishments."

Jim Rohn

Foundation, Guideposts, and Manifestation are your Elemental Principles; like atoms, they are your building blocks. Discipline, along with the next two Principles, Strategy and Understanding, are your Molecular Principles, vibrating collections of atoms fitting together in many different ways to ultimately form compounds. How does this relate to the universe? When Sun Tze in *Art of War* teaches, "He who is reckless can be killed," he is saying someone who is reckless has put himself at risk and is emphasizing the need for discipline as discipline allows for us to use the consistent stable foundation we work so hard to build. Regardless of whether it is family, work, or exercise, we need to be disciplined. Most importantly, we need to be disciplined in staying connected to source or goodness all the time! In order to do this we have to understand how we create and maintain discipline in our life. What do we need to do to have the type of discipline that will attract or accomplish what we desire?

We must use our effective habits and discipline to manifest what we desire. In order to create and maintain effective habits, it takes the integration of three things: knowledge, skill and desire. The knowledge part is easy. We gain situational knowledge just by living but we also have this book and other instructional guides. We develop skills through situational knowledge or experience, which is different than straight academic knowledge; we must practice our skills, not simply read about them. There are skills that you will need in order to succeed, such as, business skills used in negotiations, like The Press, as will be discussed, or the skill of "Don't go into a sale if you're not ready to walk away." And, of course, having the desire is completely up to you. Just watch what happens with practice and repetition if you work on these daily. So long as you live "above the line" and don't lie to yourself, you can become disciplined.

DISCIPLINE PRINCIPLE – KEY ELEMENT #1: EFFECTIVE HABITS

Effective habits are critical. They come from self-actualization and analysis. They are the foundation for your discipline. That said, we know from experience that it is extremely difficult to change bad habits and create good habits. They simply follow the laws of the universe. Bad habits feel good in the short term, but in the long term, tend to be more destructive. Vice versa, good habits tend to prove more difficult in the short term, but are more fulfilling in the long run. Consider someone going out for their first five mile run. What initially proves to be a painful experience becomes rewarding with time. Conversely, cocaine use may feel great initially, but three years later, you will definitely regret the day you started. Obviously, an awareness needs to occur to distinguish a good habit from a bad habit, and you continually need self-analysis in order to make the determination. But once something becomes a good habit, we do it without even thinking about it. It becomes ingrained and part of our lives.

> "Watch your thoughts, they become words.
> Watch your words, they become actions.
> Watch your actions, they become habits.
> Watch your habits, they become your character.
> Watch your character, it becomes your destiny."
> Unknown

In life, as in business, creating good habits or changing from bad ones requires hard work in three areas – knowledge, skills and desire – and the integration of these three determine our habits and can create the discipline that we need. Knowledge is the "what to" and the "why to" create or change. Skills are the "how to" create or change. Desire is the "want to" create or change and is the most important. It encompasses the "free will" to connect to source.

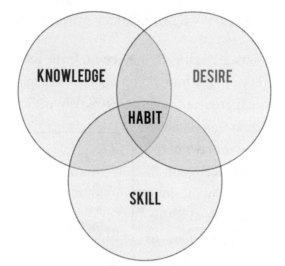

To reiterate, it can be a difficult, usually painful process to change, as change needs to be motivated by a higher purpose and a willingness to subordinate the lesser thing you want now for the greater thing you can obtain later. Do I drink too much? Am I the right weight? Do I exercise enough? Is it something I need to cut out completely, or do I honestly have control and a good balance? We also have to understand that we exist in an abundant universe, and if we focus in on what we don't have or what we can't do, this is exactly what we will manifest. Don't think of how hard it is to quit smoking, picture yourself happy and smoke free. Let this be attracted to you!

As Sidney Madwed writes:

> "The motivation for all personal behavior is to produce a sense of 'FEEL GOOD', a sense of inner peace and well-being. To expect a person to go against his desire to feel good or as good as he can feel under any momentary condition is illogical and irrational. In the observation of human behavior, one will notice every human act is a response to a personal need. This is true whether one signs a million dollar contract, scratches one's nose, rolls over in bed, or just daydreams his life away. People will do

things which seem contrary to this concept, but the bottom line is they perceive some kind of payoff which will make them feel good. And the payoff is almost always emotional. When you ask people why they want to be financially independent, they might say that they could buy things without having to worry about where the money will come from. And when they worry, they don't FEEL GOOD. A drug addict, a compulsive eater, an alcoholic and anyone with a compulsive habit will continue with their habits because at the moment of action they believe and feel it will make them feel good. That is why breaking compulsive habits are so difficult."

When I was fourteen I began chewing tobacco. As a ballplayer, it was part of the culture, and I really loved it. Unfortunately, I could not stop the chemical addiction. Until I made the decision based on a higher purpose – my wife, my kids, my health – that I no longer wanted this as a part of my life, I was able to give it up. I did not want to lose five years of being with my wife and kids (although Julie told me that the universe was

> "Habits – the only reason they persist is that they are offering some satisfaction. You allow them to persist by not seeking any other, better form of satisfying the same needs. Every habit, good or bad, is acquired and learned in the same way – by finding that it is a means of satisfaction."
>
> Juliene Berk

going to reward me for chewing tobacco because I would no longer be able to speak, so she was going to have to speak for me…Cancel). I can't even carry around the energy that I once loved chewing tobacco because a situation might arise where my guard is down and I might indulge (If only there could be a balance, like the universe, where you could engage sometimes, it would be different, but then it wouldn't be categorized as a habit, would it?). To change, you need to appreciate the energy of *why* to quit more than the energy of engaging in that habit.

Conversely, I believe that it is just as easy to be addicted to (or attract into my life) positive instead of negative things, so you may as well have a psychology of effective habits. Be aware of what habits you have. Accept them. Own them. If the habit is not something you want, use discipline to change it. Constantly explore what knowledge, desire and skill set you have to achieve whatever it is you want, and assuming you've dealt with your ego and remain accountable, you're ready to go.

One of the most effective habits that we can develop is how to maximize our time. So many desires are squashed because we end up disconnecting to source due to our time expectation. We need to create the habit of trusting the universe and know that all things will come in their own time. For example, with all the trials and tribulations that my partner Warren Moon had to endure to be the First African American Quarterback in the Pro Football Hall of Fame, we still see bias and prejudice toward black quarterbacks, or, more globally, black leaders. Warren, who I have nicknamed "QB1 Kenobi", has the wisdom that change takes time. He remains positive and appreciates the progress while he continues to work toward excellence.

> "It is good to have an end to journey toward; but it is the journey that matters, in the end."
>
> Ernest Hemingway

The difference or subtlety is the idea of thinking backwards from the end result you want to manifest and letting the means and the journey be the ultimate fulfillment with purpose. If this is your focus, the result will be manifested and the accompanying *hardware* will follow. For example, a team that wants to win the Super Bowl needs to work as a team, trust each other and the universe, and do everything they can do with positive energy. Winning the Super Bowl is the vision. Aligned with Teddy Roosevelt's thoughts in *The Strenuous Life*, the Principles in this book are the means to that end with the struggle and strife and what is overcome along the way leading to fulfillment. On the other hand, if the team's end is the Super Bowl ring, which the winning players receive, I would argue that this is a misplaced or misguided result. The ring is the ego disconnecting us from source telling us, "I can walk around and people will think highly of me because I have a Super Bowl ring." The silly thing about awards is that you can actually buy most of them on eBay without ever having earned them! The purpose and fulfillment of the achievement is the end, not the accolade or awards which will inevitably come with determined focus.

I lost sight of this concept when I manifested my golf course. I was so busy letting people know that *Golf Digest* named it one of the eight best new golf courses in the country that I failed to see the achievement in building a truly spiritual place that many could enjoy. I wanted my ego stroked with accolades and an enhancement of my reputation when, instead, I should have appreciated the golf course and used my energy to continue to make the golf course thrive. Again, there is no way to happiness and fulfillment. Fulfillment and happiness are the way.

I know about being disconnected from source and unhappy from the experience. When I was at the supposed pinnacle of my career, for the first time, I felt empty. I spoke to Paul Allen formerly of Microsoft, who I consider a mentor of mine from the tech sector, after he gave a speech similar in content to the advice I am sharing with respect to the most important good habit of connecting to and staying connected to source energy or goodness. Paul had a similar story. He made a fortune

> "Zoo: An excellent place to study the habits of human beings."
> Evan Esar

with Microsoft and was seemingly at the pinnacle of his career, yet he was not happy. Like me, the more successful he appeared in other people's eyes, the emptier he felt. Paul went out and bought things, but these things didn't make him happy. So he bought more things and different things, and still no happiness. Then a friend delivering wheelchairs to the Middle East invited him along. As he was delivering the chairs to many injured women and children, a four-year-old boy ran up to him with tears in his eyes, thanking him profusely for the chair he had delivered. It would finally allow his mother, injured when he was an infant, to leave her bed. Paul looked at me with tears in his eyes and said it was at that point that he finally felt happy. Simply stated, when we connect to goodness, we feel happy or good! So make it a habit to feel good by doing good!

Discipline Principle – Key Element #2: Performance

The correlation between performance and morale must be understood.

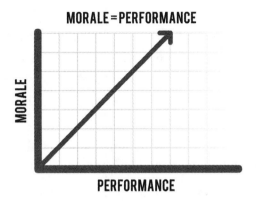

They are directly related. Generally and quite simply, we perform well when we "feel good" or are connected to source or goodness (thus the correlation between good, goodness and source in all religions) and perform poorly when we feel bad or are not connected, or have a corroded connection. Now add the notion that the only one who knows your performance is you; you are the only one who lives with yourself all of the time. Morale or, as I like to call it, our internal energy or emotion becomes the key factor regarding performance and its sustainability over time. It is all a perception of how you feel. In fact, the perception of morale as directly related to performance is also a good habit to develop.

We don't think about creating or maintaining effective habits all the time, but two habits directly affect our performance and morale. Think about them when you're feeling really great so that you can remind yourself what it feels like in order to create the chemical reactions in your brain. To replicate it and manifest that feeling constantly, you want to duplicate or clone the positive energy of what it feels like to be connected.

Habit #1: Become aware of what it feels like to be connected to goodness or source.

Habit #2: Think about Habit #1 when you're not feeling good in order to get yourself back on track with that memorized feeling.

Be aware of when this happens. In other words you need to be aware of when you are connected and not connected as this is essential to manifesting what you desire. You need to continually utilize the AAA Strategy with the universe to Align, take Action, and Adjust, and awareness is essential to do this. Liken it to golf and hitting that perfect drive. Once you hit it, you then want to do it again and again and again.

Have you ever seen a sports team win based on momentum? Remember the Jim McMahon example from the Preface. The Bears won because they had great morale and their performance was extreme. This is an excellent example of how individual manifestations that scale to others can then become a collective belief or energy for a more global effect. Indeed, the greatest athletes are the ones who play at a high level for a long time. The best business people will be the ones who create abundance

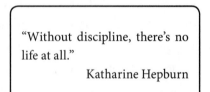

"Without discipline, there's no life at all."

Katharine Hepburn

consistently over a long period of time. This high sustainability of performance is often attributable to morale, awareness and accountability of "living above the line" and staying connected or keeping your connection clean. You can only control yourself, and it's your own self-carried inner energy that sometimes contradicts how you think about yourself, or that you may be in denial about. You're the only one who can make yourself feel bad (when you are disconnected). No one but you can deal with your own insecurities. The whole universe is in your head, between your ears – the most valuable six inches of your universe. So when things go right or go wrong, look between your ears. This is why it's so important to meditate, look self-reflectively, and listen when you continually hear the same response from others, see the same things, feel the same way, or think the same thoughts. Learn how to stay connected to goodness and cancel the negative energy.

But what if your performance and morale are suffering and "Cancel" does not seem to be enough? How can you connect back to goodness or source? You can get out of your own way by taking some time to clear the negativity and then move forward. You wouldn't try to drive a car without gas, after all, would you? Take some time and get connected with clarity before coming back, rather than trying to plow through and getting in your own way.

When I was running the sales force at West Publishing, I would have sales representatives call me with low morale. I'd tell them to stop working and go to the beach, and no, I wasn't in Minnesota in the middle of the winter, but in Southern California at the time. Not realizing it then, I was actually telling them to only return to work when they were clear, balanced, and focused, and connected back to source. I'd point out to them that they'd get nothing productive done and would end up damaging business relationships. I'd rather have them spend their free will connecting to source and goodness instead of them being in their own way and try to force something that was not going to happen because of them putting out the wrong energy based on their low morale, regardless of the reason.

> "Performance is your reality. Forget everything else."
> Harold Geneen

Basically then, when you're experiencing a bad connection or are completely disconnected, you need to get your connection clean, or reconnect, before doing anything else. But again, that connection is up to you, in the same way that feeling bad for other people does not make them feel good. My connection is irrelevant to your free will to connect or not, and even if you are connected to goodness or source and tell me you're sick, the only way I can help you is to pray for your health and happiness because I'll never feel sick enough to heal you. You simply can't change someone else's circumstance by looking at them differently. Only *they* can change the way they look at things and, if they do, the things they look at will change.

If I tell someone their eyes are unattractive and they, themselves, believe their eyes are beautiful, they will merely chuckle. If, however, I tell someone they are overweight and that person is insecure, they may suffer from hurt feelings. But this has nothing to do with me other than the fact that I am putting negative energy toward something that this person is attracting with their own negative energy, or this person is projecting their own insecurity about this issue. Remember, I can't define anyone else. All I'm defining is me and my thoughts and words, which best not be negative lest I attract that negativity into my own life. In other words, negative energy will only have an effect if that person is receptive to it. The universe works in harmony, so if you're

> "Success in business requires training and discipline and hard work. But if you're not frightened by these things, the opportunities are just as great today as they ever were."
> David Rockefeller

connected to goodness, the negative energy doesn't even exist. If you and the other person are connected to goodness, nothing hurtful will be said and/or nothing hurtful will be attracted and/or anything hurtful will be of no harm.

Knowing this, you can use it to motivate people in business. The biggest insecurity of a buyer, for example, is having to admit that he/she can't afford something. What needs to be done as a seller is to create the energy to help the buyer find the funds, and put them at ease by explaining the critical business issues that they're facing, then motivate them that this will build abundance for them even if it hurts or is challenging in the short term. You become their consultant, part of their vision … it's simple math. We need to help them connect to source.

To summarize performance and morale, it is about being connected and staying connected. You must know yourself and keep your own emotions or morale high by manifesting what you desire, and creating your own connection to source. It happens by taking the power of your energy in motion or emotions and staying connected. It happens by duplicating the good stuff and eradicating the bad stuff. Remember, the journey is the fun part. The harder you work and the more valuable the objectives are to you, the better you'll feel when you achieve them. The easier it comes, the easier it goes, be it money, be it a job. Thus, compel yourself to have good morale or to stay connected to source or goodness. Compel yourself to continue to have good performance, to put your effective habits in place. Be disciplined so that if you have negative feelings, you can cancel, shift your energy, and connect back to goodness. You can live a fulfilled existence, creating more positive energy, which, in turn, will attract even greater energy.

> "I realized I could run after finding out that my dad used to run and it gave me the morale that if he did it then maybe I could also run."
>
> David Rudisha

Discipline Principle – Key Element #3: Penn Value

I will use the case study that I've taught around the world to illustrate Penn Value. I ask my students if they believe that, in less than a minute, I could sell them a plastic pen for a million dollars even though it appears to be the same pen you can buy at Walmart for .39 cents.

Before you scoff, like they usually do, hear me out.

First, I will give you a no interest loan for a million dollars. Then, I am going to create a one million dollar escrow account with a guarantee of execution by your lawyer that states if you buy this pen for the million dollar no-interest loan and you cannot sell this pen for two million after twelve months, I will relieve you of your one million dollar debt and the money from the escrow account will be immediately released to you. And you get to keep the pen!

Under this scenario, can you see any reason you wouldn't want to buy this .39 cent pen? I've made certain that if you buy the pen for $1 million dollars, along with the mechanism and empowerment to do so, you have the guaranteed opportunity to make $2 million dollars with a certainty of not losing a cent yourself and gaining, at least, $1 million dollars (and a free pen). The point is here's a product that is obviously not worth $1 million dollars, but even if faced with reluctance or hesitation, if you can effectively communicate a value, you can sell anything. Whether it fits within someone's Foundations is a completely different story; I had one intern who said she'd decline the offer because she'd be stressed by having $1 million dollars.

But following the Principles and Key Elements, my objective is to always lead the other party to the logical conclusion of "Can you see any reason why we shouldn't move forward?" In this case, why wouldn't they want to buy the pen? It's risk-free. Or more properly stated, it is a completely abundant business situation with a very high Penn Value.

Life is about choices and putting the correct energy toward valuing these choices. When we make decisions about what we desire, we must be connected to goodness. Since the universe is abundant, when you give "X" amount of value, how certain will you be to receive equal or greater value? Most of us will put in the energy or work if

> "Discipline is the soul of an army. It makes small numbers formidable, procures success to the weak, and esteem to all."
>
> George Washington

we believe it will scale and we'll get benefit from it. Conversely, if we believe the universe is scarce, very few will act knowing that it will result in a loss of energy or value. This is applicable in business and life whether we are receiving or giving our energy or value.

For example, if I give money to an individual on a street corner seeking food, it does not matter to me if that individual later uses my donation for liquor. When I decided that I wanted to fulfill part of my giving value and fulfill the universe by donating the money, I have done what I have believed in within my personal values and I will, in fact, receive something back. I trust the universe, and by betting on the universe, I will, in turn, be a good bet of the universe regardless of whether the person on the corner conned me or not. I am accountable for me and my intentions of connecting to goodness.

You need to value and be accountable and aware of everything you do, which entails utilizing the Key Elements of these Seven Principles. Everything you do in life has a value to it. This is how you make your decisions. For example, I had to utilize Penn Value to create the discipline not to chew tobacco; until I could create the value of not using over the value of using chewing tobacco (meaning the joy of tobacco use over my wife speaking for me the rest of my life), none of it mattered regardless of what discipline I had.

Further, whenever you make a decision in your life, you have to prioritize your values. For example, often when we invite people to our children's birthday parties, some people can't make it. In this same situation, many hosts will take offense for someone choosing to do something other than attending. We need to stay connected and feeling abundant, and realize that there's simply something that others are giving more priority to, or they would have come. The reason does not matter! Time is the most valuable

> "The body is shaped, disciplined, honored, and in time, trusted."
> Martha Graham

thing we have, and too many people take too great of an offense when others choose not to spend it with them. That's why, in general, it's so important how and with whom you spend your time.

When you are confident and connected in business, you'll maximize your leverage in your own sales effort, either as a buyer or a seller. As a buyer, you can almost always return to an opportunity. Remember, you have the leverage because you have the money. Money is a very powerful energy because of what it represents. Go around a room and ask people what money means to them and you'll hear concepts like "Security" and "Freedom". So, it's not so much what money can buy, but what energy money carries. I participated in a very interesting workshop that demonstrated the effects of both an abundance and a scarcity of money. They gave all twenty of us in the room twenty gold pieces each. With Pink Floyd's song *Money* blaring,

"Money-Money-Money-Money!", the object of the first exercise was, after hiding your own gold pieces, to collect (grab) as many as you could within an allotted time. In the second exercise, you had to give away as many of your gold pieces as you could within the same allotted time as a Kool & The Gang's *Celebration* played in the background. The difference in energy between the two exercises was amazing. The first, the money grab, was frenetic and stressful to the "nth" Power, with the time seeming to be running out as compared to the second. The money giveaway, with the sharing of abundance, felt relaxing and enjoyable with no pressure whatsoever.

> "Learn the art of patience. Apply discipline to your thoughts when they become anxious over the outcome of a goal. Impatience breeds anxiety, fear, discouragement and failure. Patience creates confidence, decisiveness, and a rational outlook, which eventually leads to success."
>
> Brian Adams

Because you have the leverage and the energy of having the money, anything worth negotiating for – a car, a home – I would suggest walking away from for a day. And walk away saying "No", "Sorry", "It's not worth it" – not "I'll think about it". Watch how quickly people will chase after you. If you lose the deal, you simply trust that the universe will attract that which is the most abundant for you. Trust the universe to create the most efficient and best circumstances for you, be it the best price, best value, best home, best car. And if those business situations bring challenges, just be excited about the lessons, growth, and benefit of the journey to come.

Now that I've said this, is there anything a seller can do in this situation in an attempt to keep that buyer from walking away? To maximize your statistical success, you, the seller will need to work through stimulating their interest correctly, transitioning that interest, sharing their vision, giving them Penn Value, and most of all, managing and developing that vision to thrive. The bottom line is that if someone is 100% sure that they'll make more money or get more of what they want for less than they're giving, they will move forward 100% of the time. They may act as if they're willing to walk, but trust the universe that if you've created the value, they'll be right back because you've created an abundant business situation where there's no reason not to move forward.

Yes, the previous example makes sense purely on a monetary level, but hopefully you're now starting to take your analysis to a greater level. How will the extra dollars affect you, your health, and your family? How will it affect your character, integrity and discipline? Will it create more or less good experiences or positive energy? And if you

> "Nothing of value is free. Even the breath of life is purchased at birth only through gasping effort and pain."
>
> Robert A. Heinlein

get the money, how much do you spend and how much do you sock away for your three-year-old's college education?

This is what Penn Value is all about. Many lottery winners, professional athletes, and other "entitled" or self-entitled people, soon end up bankrupt. They have no discipline, they have acquired bad habits or have no effective habits, they don't understand that morale is tied to performance, but most of all, they don't understand Penn Value. If they did, they'd say to all the people who want to borrow money, "I'm not your bank, and I owe you nothing. I'm more than happy to help you, but only with working out a business plan to attain it through your own efforts." Throughout my journey of happiness and fulfillment, I lost millions because I didn't employ Penn Value to my life, and it was one of the most valuable, rewarding and best things that ever happened to me. I would not have found the path to true happiness otherwise.

Let's distinguish Penn Value and abundance from the idea of something "too good to be true". With me, my own business pitch evolved to the point where I became so masterful that instead of the other party agreeing every time, they began asking, "What's the catch?" Then I had to scale the pitch back so that it did not appear to be too good to be true. I was going over the value limit. This is a common mistake of "eagles" or natural born sales people. They're gifted with the ability to share a vision and energy. When it comes to business, they're connected and can inspire others quickly. The dangers associated to being an "eagle" are similar to those of an "Arriver", someone who I will be describing in much greater depth later.

The biggest fault of eagles is overselling or back-end selling. Overselling, in this sense, means exaggerating in some way or another. Back-end selling means misrepresenting something upfront that the seller knows he or she can

> "Greatness is more than potential. It is the execution of that potential. Beyond the raw talent. You need the appropriate training. You need the discipline. You need the inspiration. You need the drive."
>
> Eric A. Burns

counteract on the back end of a deal. This is usually based on a seller's experience and statistical analysis. An example of back-end selling would be if I sold you a new car and charged you extra for rust protection which I don't actually provide knowing that for 99% of the population rust won't develop for six years. In six years, I know statistically that either most people will no longer own that vehicle, or I might not care, knowing that I probably will have moved on to another job by that time, thereby sticking someone else with that customer's problem should rust develop. If it so happens that I am still working at the dealership and the customer comes in with rust, I would feign oversight: "Oh, someone must not have noticed that on the bill of sale, but let's take care of the rust right now."

Quite often, eagles can get away with both overselling and back-end selling. If you're an eagle, you need to be aware of this and you need to scale it back by staying connected to goodness. A good way to know if you are overselling is if after the sale and during the management of the vision people are telling you, "This is not what you promised me, I'm not quite satisfied, you haven't exceeded my expectations," or returning to the initial premise, that what they heard was indeed too good to be true. If you do business correctly, you'll stay connected and your business will grow to the "nth" Power. I promise you that if it sounds too good to be true, it is! This is not just my opinion. Physics, math, psychology and philosophy all say it is. There's always a catch. Why do you think it's so easy to start that "free" subscription and hard to cancel it?

But people love the word "free". The word "free" carries an energy with it. In a business sense, in a business deal, nothing is ever "free".

> "Seek freedom and become captive of your desires, seek discipline and find your liberty."
>
> Frank Herbert

"Free" does not mean "no money". When I receive a purportedly "free" product from a sponsor or potential sponsor, these people are getting value from us having and utilizing their product. In fact, sometimes the value to the sponsor or potential sponsor exceeds the product's value to us, all gauged by the Penn Value.

So, in a business sense, make sure you're selling only what's true or by making sure that you stay connected to goodness or source. The only time I would suggest making something sound too good to be true is when you are attempting to stimulate someone's interest in that something because, at this point, you're really doing nothing more than motivating them to share a vision, and you can utilize the AAA Strategy to make sure the vision is aligned and connected to source. But once you're in that vision, it needs to be true and connected to goodness. You need to be able to perform or deliver more than you promise.

Finally, in case you are wondering why I give the pen example, yet spell "Penn" with two Ns, Penn is my wife's maiden name. I always like to let her know that I'm thinking of her, and honoring her, by naming something after her (although she'd probably like something more significant). Regardless, it helps keep my foundation solid and she has brought me the most value to my life!

> "There is no discipline in the world so severe as the discipline of experience subjected to the tests of intelligent development and direction."
>
> John Dewey

Discipline Principle – Key Element #4:
The Ben Franklin Effect

The summer before I left for college my mother made me read a book. That book was Ben Franklin's autobiography. As you can imagine, I was not at all pleased with my mother. I wanted to spend my time at the beach and working out for my first year of college football. As usual, though, I am so grateful that my mother empowered me with this gift of enlightenment. In his autobiography, Ben Franklin teaches that the best thing someone can do is to ask for help. If you ask someone for help, you become an investment of that person. Now, you have two people aligned with your energy and vision. Two people are now attracting like-kind energy.

> "Tell me and I forget. Teach me and I remember. Involve me and I learn."
>
> Benjamin Franklin

For example, when I started college, I implemented the wisdom that I had gleaned from reading Ben Franklin's book and moved everything in my syllabus up one week, enabling me to hand in papers a week early. As I turned those papers in, I'd tell my professors that my objective was to achieve straight As, I'd do whatever it took to get an A, and that I had finished my paper early in order for the professor to see if I was on the right track. In effect, this almost guaranteed me an A on many levels. The professor knew I was invested and connected. The professor knew that we'd be aligned with our objectives and, in the end, I'd turn in a paper that was a combination of my ideas aligned with what she/he wanted. And I promise you, I wasn't any smarter than anyone else in the class.

Interestingly, Ben Franklin also said, "He that has once done you a kindness will be more ready to do you another than he whom you yourself have obliged." In other words, if you do them a favor once, you are more apt to do them another favor. It may seem counterintuitive, but, psychologically, you have so much invested, you become obliged. It becomes Ben Franklin to the "nth" Power. When people get in the habit of helping you, and you get into the habit of helping others, the energy of it continues on and multiplies. This is because you have engineered a situation where not only are you connected to goodness, but you have helped your business client or other person to connect. When we do a

> "I didn't fail the test, I just found 100 ways to do it wrong."
> Benjamin Franklin

person a favor, we tend to like them more as a result. This is because we justify our actions to ourselves, that we did them a favor because we liked them.

The opposite, better known as "The Reverse Ben Franklin Effect", also works. For example, in business, what if you meet resistance in attempting to get alignment or share a vision? In this case, use the AAA Strategy to see if you can reengineer the vision for your potential business client. But if you get resistance three times after using the AAA Strategy, including making the necessary Adjustments, reengineer the vision by implementing the Ben Franklin Effect or the Reverse. Most people quit on the business too early instead of being more interested than interesting and exploring the reasons, impact and capabilities involved. Obviously, more information is needed by the other party. Emotion or value hasn't been effectively communicated, or the time may not be right. For example, regardless of energy or approach, the best business person in the world with the greatest deal going will not be able to move forward with an individual whose mother just died. So, after hearing "No" for the third time, say, "This obviously isn't a good time," with the right emotion or value. Then implement the Reverse Ben Franklin effect, not by asking for help, but by offering help. Simply ask, "Is there anything I can do for you?" or ask a favor of them, "Do you know anyone else who would like to utilize this?" I promise you the energy will change, and you'll become more statistically successful.

I once went to an interview for a consulting job. Beth, the person who had arranged this interview on my behalf, informed me ahead of time how difficult it had been to set up this meeting for me. Anyway, once in the room, I could tell almost immediately that the energy of the person interviewing me was way off. In fact, before we even started discussing the consulting job, I asked him, "Is everything okay? Is there anything I can do for you?"

> "He that is good for making excuses is seldom good for anything else."
> Benjamin Franklin

It turned out he was going through a tough time personally. We ended up just talking and never even got around to discussing the consulting job. Later that day, Beth asked me whether or not I had been offered the job. I informed her that we hadn't discussed the position at all. Beth was then, well, let's politely say fairly pissed at me, reiterating how hard it had been to set up the interview. But the next day, I received another phone call from Beth. She was a bit perplexed that the gentleman I'd met with for the consulting job had just called her and wanted to hire me regardless of the fact we never even discussed the job.

The moral of the story: in business, stay connected to goodness, don't lose sight of the big picture, and incorporate both Ben Franklin Effects. Ask the other party questions like, "Can you see any reason you wouldn't want to go forward with this?", "Can you help me with this?", and "What else can you do?" But always take it to the next step to create a thriving business, and in order to avoid having any negative energy attracted to you or your business. Therefore, always ask, "Is there anything I can do for you?" Even if I don't get what I want when I want it, I always ask, "Is there anything I can do for you?"

It is important to understand the Ben Franklin Effect because you need to be disciplined to look for and give help. Stay connected to source and goodness to create abundance for everyone.

By utilizing the Ben Franklin Effects of asking for and offering help, along with making sure you say "thank you", people will feel obliged and will help again. The more you ask for help, the more you give help, and the more grateful you are for both, the better off you will be. Help yourself and help others connect by staying connected to goodness.

> "Many people die at twenty-five and aren't buried until they are seventy-five."
>
> Benjamin Franklin

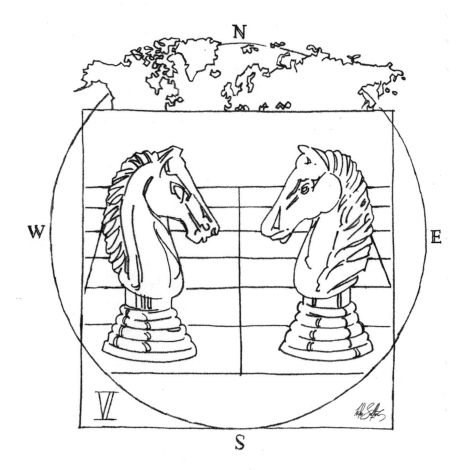

V. PRINCIPLE FIVE: STRATEGY

"There's only one growth strategy: work hard."

William Hague

Okay, how do you now use all of the Principles and the Keys that you've learned? The answer is Strategy. Before I became enlightened, I agreed with William Hague. I believed that all it took was hard work and that I would simply outwork you. As you know, I ended up putting a lot of velocity into an unstable foundation. Instead, now that you'll be able to accomplish your dreams with your Foundation, Guideposts, Manifestation and Discipline firmly in place, developing a Strategy, through knowledge, planning, emotion (or, as I call it, energy in motion) and effective communication, will help you to maximize your results.

STRATEGY PRINCIPLE – KEY ELEMENT #1: KNOWLEDGE

Knowledge is truly power. Mental waves are the strongest energy in the universe. They're the only things that vibrate faster than ourselves, light or sound. Science has demonstrated that if you talk nicely to water – "I love you water and you're so beautiful" – it will turn or remain clear. On the other hand, if you talk harshly to water – "I hate you water and you're so ugly" – it will actually turn brown. One can only imagine if our voices and sound have that kind of power, what kind of energy our mental waves

> "Integrity without knowledge is weak and useless, and knowledge without integrity is dangerous and dreadful."
> Samuel Johnson

and thoughts carry. Mental waves are actually measureable. I was taught that our body harnesses enough energy to light up all of Manhattan for a single day. This is why it's so important to be connected to source or goodness as well as to see what we want, because it already exists. This is also why it's so important to cancel negative thoughts. By cancelling, instead of the negativity growing or attracting, the negative energy will immediately dissipate. This is an easy way to get you back on track, connected to source and goodness. By staying connected, you'll manifest more rapidly and accurately.

Recall from Section One my uncle co-signing on my student loans so that I could finish law school; his wisdom was that if I didn't invest in myself, what was I ever going to invest in? How right he was. We all know people who've wasted the opportunity and refused to invest in themselves, and are now stuck in a situation that they know they don't want to be in. Were they afraid of success?

Invest in yourself. Invest in knowledge ... for as my mom says, "If you think education is expensive, try ignorance." The one thing someone can't take from you is your mind. Someone can take your

126

life, but your mental waves and your continued empowerment of others, and others beyond them to the "nth" Power, lives on.

Now that we agree knowledge is power, let's remember that the laws of attraction apply to power as well, thus … power attracts power. Therefore, in life and business, you want to have as much knowledge as possible to maximize your power or energy. When communicating with power, you need to make someone feel that you are worth listening to and that you can guide or help them.

Have you ever been in a conversation where you can barely finish before the other person is already better than you? They have a better story. You won twice, they won three times. You have a sailboat, they have a yacht. These are examples of the classic "One Upper". What you want to do is to make yourself equal and then distinguish yourself. This is not meant in terms of superiority, like the person with the stories in the previous example, but in making *yourself* better than you were before. By this I mean you're providing extra-value or being extra-ordinary or extraordinary. This also allows the other person to distinguish him- or herself because everybody has inherent value. The energy flows much better this way. This holds true whether you are talking about a competitive product or yourself. Make yourself equal to their value and then create a higher Penn Value. It is important to ask more open- and closed-ended questions because the more you can understand and align with the other person's value system, based on their foundation, the better the certainty of success.

> "The knowledge of the world is only to be acquired in the world, and not in a closet."
>
> Lord Chesterfield

Indeed, in order to explore anything in life and business, you need to know the reasons someone would do something, which encompasses their values, and the impact it will have on them, which encompasses their past and their vision for the future. You then need to match the reasons and impact at the highest Penn Value to the capabilities that you have. Recall the Penn Value example. I was able to take the reason someone would want to buy the pen (a risk-free guarantee of a million dollar profit), the impact the million dollars would have on them, and my capability to provide an interest-free loan and an escrow account containing another million dollars. If I understand the reasons you would do something, the impact it would have on you and how it matches my capabilities, we can get alignment on its value.

One way to obtain this information is to get someone to talk. Remember, people like to talk – especially about themselves. In law school, I learned how best to acquire information from someone. First, you ask open-ended (or non-leading) questions. These are questions that result in a broad, narrative responsive. Typically, these are the "Who", "What", "Where", "When" and "How" questions. "What kind of business do you have?" "How did you start your business?"

Then, when you have the raw data based on their response, you narrow down what an individual is saying through closed or leading questions. These are questions that suggest or provide the answer. Typically,

> "It is no good to try to stop knowledge from going forward. Ignorance is never better than knowledge."
>
> Enrico Fermi

when boiled down to its essence, the answer to a closed or leading question is a simple "Yes" or "No". In our case, the closed or leading questions will relate to the reasons for going forward, the impact it will have, or the capabilities to increase Penn Value and create alignment. "Don't you think a good reason to buy this pen is because you'll make a million dollars?" "Isn't the fact that I'm able to make this a risk-free deal for you a good thing?"

You then use a summary to confirm the alignment. Because it's not what you say, but what they hear; you want to make sure that it's their idea. Let them state the Penn Value.

Strategy Principle – Key Element #2: Planning

As Benjamin Franklin said, "By failing to prepare, you are preparing to fail." To achieve success in any endeavor, you need to have a plan. You need to think about it. You need to be more interested than interesting. You need to take the time and bring all of those things that are interconnected into the

> "Good plans shape good decisions. That's why good planning helps to make elusive dreams come true."
>
> Lester R. Bittel

equation. Create a systematic approach. Meditate, use a vision board, a to-do list, a phone or computer application, but plan and prioritize by the hour, day, month and year. I work my way from the most important, most frequent items first, then start creating systems of efficiency for each one.

For instance, brushing your teeth is an extremely important daily exercise. After I thought about it, I was able to reduce by 2/3 the time it took me to brush my teeth. I was able to cut the time it takes to brush my teeth by 2 minutes and 30 seconds. It may not seem like a lot, but when you multiply this by 365, I've just created over 21 more hours a year to spend with my kids. By utilizing this same approach of creating systems of efficiency resulting in time savings, I was able to shave ten minutes off of my entire morning process. At the end of a six-day workweek, I had an extra hour. This then gave me four extra hours a month, 52 extra hours a year. I promise you that I was still clean and dressed, and I can tell you that my wife and three daughters were happy to find the bathroom vacant. I then became even more efficient and was able to cut my morning process by another ten minutes a day, and now I had 104 more hours in a year than the average person.

I then looked at how I got to work and where I lived and, if I couldn't shave time off my commute, how I could use my car time effectively. I started having people call me or I'd call them the minute I got in my car to go to the office (using hands-free Bluetooth of course). I noticed the same thing about having lunch and decided it needed to be an effective lunch, building it around business. And of course, there's multi-tasking, but it needs to be effective multi-tasking for it to be of value. For instance, I like to watch certain things on television, like sports. If I'm watching sports on television, I think about what else I can also be doing, like folding my clothes. So long as you are in a peaceful place, you could also stretch in the morning while meditating (I meditate at least twenty minutes every morning in order for everything to come to me and for me to gain greater awareness). The point is consciously consider those activities where you can effectively do two or even three things at once.

> "In preparing for battle I have always found that plans are useless, but planning is indispensable."
>
> Dwight D. Eisenhower

Now that you've become more efficient by planning, you can take it one step further and achieve up to 64 hours of production in a day over the average person. How is that possible? Stay with me: most people work eight hours a day. But in those eight hours, are people truly efficient? Believe it or not, between the water cooler, lunches, banter, the Internet, texting, the phone, there is only about two hours of production in an eight hour day ... if lucky. With my own system in place, I, personally, work and do all that I need to do sixteen hours a day. And based on my Principles and Keys, I know that I'm twice as efficient as the average person.

Now that you are aware of your Principles and Keys, you can then increase your statistical success. For example, in business, if you previously had success with one out of every ten business calls, you become twice as productive when you can increase that success to two out of every ten calls. Conceivably, if you are like me, you're now up to sixty-four hours of production over the average person in a day (16 hours of work a day x twice the efficiency of production as compared to the norm x twice the productivity compared to the norm = 64 hours of production a day over the normal person working one eight hour day).

8 HOUR AVERAGE WORKDAY
X 2 (TWICE THE HOURS)
X 2 (TWICE THE EFFICIENCY)
X 2 (TWICE THE STATISTICAL SUCCESS)

= 64 HOURS OF PRODUCTION

Talk about velocity! Imagine what you could do in a five-day workweek? If you can imagine that, well, I work six days a week. Assuming everything else, like stability, is in place and balanced, this is how you become successful and are able to manifest what you desire faster and more accurately. Yes, it takes planning, but you'll accomplish more before 8:30 a.m. than most people will accomplish all day … yet, you'll find that you will be at peace.

Lest you think I didn't or don't spend time with my family, remember that they are an important part of my personal values and that I strive to maintain a healthy balance. I use the same exact Principles and Keys to make sure that I have quality time with my wife and kids. When I am with them, most times I focus my attention solely on them and always try to be more interested than interesting. I help teach and empower them and we all thrive. It's also important to realize that at times you can multi-task with your family as well. For example, my daughters are all competitive cheerleaders and, although the competitions take an entire weekend and my daughters are only on stage a total of ten minutes, it's still extremely important that I be present. Most of my time is actually spent with my wife and son, and even working on my laptop, but I'm showing my daughters support and giving my full attention when it matters. I actually have a plan for each weekend for my family, friends, and fun, just as I have a plan for work!

You'll discover added benefits to planning as well. Going on four years now, I still print out a calendar despite the fact that I'm tech savvy. A copy of the calendar travels with me and another copy stays on my desk. It may not seem a great effort, but I've trained myself and now have the good habit of glancing at the calendar before every half hour. So, at 8:55 a.m., I'll look to see what I have at 9:00 a.m. and so on. Now, not only have my events been planned out, but I have gained respect, credibility and a reputation for my timeliness and an ability to stay on schedule. I don't forget calls and am always conscious to move on to the next thing.

> "Men often oppose a thing merely because they have had no agency in planning it, or because it may have been planned by those whom they dislike."
>
> Alexander Hamilton

In business, effective planning also encompasses pre-qualification. How do you pre-qualify something? You do research, think, and evaluate. You look at and organize possible entities you may want to approach by individuals, businesses, industries, affiliates, partnerships. There are so many categories that companies can fit into. For example, consider the company's size and revenue. Depending on, for instance, the value of the product or service that you're selling, you'll be statistically more successful with different types of categorized companies, and there are different independent variables that will be more or less important to this statistical success. If you're selling a software license, you'll be looking for a company with a great number of employees. If you're looking to sell something that will cost $250,000 in system integration, you're looking to approach a Fortune 500 company. If you're looking for some products and $500 for a baseball video, you have a much larger pool of prospects. But you might also find that this opportunity's sales cycle may be much longer with a larger company, so you may want to focus on smaller companies with more streamlined decision-making processes instead.

So when pre-qualifying, be more interested than interesting and dig. Obviously, we've been blessed with the great gift of search engines like Google, Bing and

> "Adventure is just bad planning."
> Roald Amundsen

Yahoo. In my opinion, search engines replicate the universe; so if you put something out there, let the universe act like a search engine and attract what you need. And like the universe, the more specific the search, the better the results. Reverse engineer with the reasons, impact and capabilities to pre-qualify and determine your categories of focus, and to determine where to place your energy and where that energy will be most attracted. Determine who and where your market is.

For example, if I was a woman trying to expose an opportunity to get married, I'm going to start doing some due diligence to find out where rich, single, middle-aged men go. Maybe I learn it's the Century Plaza Hotel and that if I hang out at the bar there, every day, I'd meet ten different, interesting men from around the country. Or if I'm selling a very specific item that has a very specific purpose, like a breast pump that works in half the time with half the discomfort at half the price, there's a certain demographic for stimulating interest or attracting that exact prospect. I will then pre-qualify by organizations, regions, age, sex, pregnancy status or likelihood of getting pregnant, number of children, hospitals and the like. Through my due diligence, I may learn about an organization with a website that 30,000 women visit three months before birth for information on breastfeeding. This will be an organization that I'll approach.

If I was selling lifts in shoes, height would be a huge category, and I'd want to find where the people who are 5-feet 7-inches and under are located. These are all eclectic examples of what you can manifest if you pre-qualify with accuracy in order to attract what you desire.

Obviously, look for the lowest hanging fruit – where do you or someone you know have connections to the lowest hanging fruit that makes obvious sense to approach based on what you're trying to sell. You'll have the greatest statistical success with this relationship capital and be able to manifest what you desire in this sales context.

We are always qualifying and pre-qualifying for the next steps as part of planning. You should constantly be aware of

> "I get up every morning determined to both change the world and have one hell of a good time. Sometimes this makes planning my day difficult."
>
> E. B. White

what you are attracting. I'll advise people: "Imagine yourself in the position with the circumstances or situation that you wish you were in." I cannot begin to tell you how often people who have approached me said, for instance, that they hate their job flipping burgers and want to be pursing their passion working with children and sports. Then they've returned after heeding my advice and embracing my Principles with the news that, from seemingly out of nowhere, a job opened up to work with children at a sports training facility … and usually for greater pay. And I also can't tell you how many times I've found a book that's been sitting on my shelf for years that had the perfect message for me right when I needed it.

The first step in planning is to see it in your mind's eye – know what it is that you *really* want by continually thinking and focusing on it – and you will attract it. Then from out of the blue, when you have a clean connection between you and source, something will give you that "ah-ha!" moment, that idea, that inspiration. And the cleaner the connection, the less corrosion, the quicker and more accurate the attraction will be. As always, as this is true in life, this is also true in business. Pre-qualifying or planning is ultimately just another term for focusing on and attracting what you desire.

> "When I was overweight and unhappy, I thought about being smaller, I thought about fitting into different clothes and feeling comfortable in any environment or social situation. But I didn't do anything about it. I was letting myself fall victim to not planning, not clarifying steps to reach my goals. Don't go on just wanting something. Start consciously planning where you want to be."
>
> Ali Vincent

STRATEGY PRINCIPLE – KEY ELEMENT #3: EMOTION

The bottom line in business is that people sell to people, people buy from people. Emotion is nothing more than energy in motion. This is why we can read something in a book or see something on television and start to cry. Just witnessing an important event or picture can be emotionally overwhelming. We are all vibrating energy beings; electricity even flows through our DNA and our body is a conduit, with 80% of our body made of water. This is why we feel things that we call emotions, through our own or other people's thoughts. Be aware of what moves you and align with it. Don't hold your emotions in. Don't resist your emotions or block them. Personally, I believe that most divorces result from this very problem. Rather than dealing with their emotions and the underlying issues, rather than

> "Where we have strong emotions, we're liable to fool ourselves."
> Carl Sagan

releasing the energy in order to realign with their partner, either or both individuals block their emotions until they build to such an extent that the damage done is irreversible. In an extreme example, one of my best friend's mom, who never even argued with her spouse, woke up and rolled over one morning after thirty years of marriage and told her husband she was miserable and wanted a divorce.

Blocking your emotions will definitely corrode your connection to goodness or source. If you don't share your emotions, you won't receive either. Where we block the flow, there is no energy in motion, which is the essence of emotions (to the contrary, you have stagnant energy). And remember what you resist persists! So don't block, stay connected and set your energy in motion. Contemplate the reasons, impacts and capabilities that hide beneath the emotions you are feeling. To be emotional is fine at the right moments. Other times, though, emotions, or perhaps I should say, negative emotions can affect things like your stability, which affects your foundation and so on. It is all about the timing of utilizing emotions.

For negotiation or motivational purposes, sometimes the best course of action is to draw upon emotions, while, at other times, detachment is the best route to follow. Another way to look at this is "How do I put my energy in motion to connect to source or goodness?" Being aware and understanding your own emotions, using the habit of saying or thinking "Cancel" (or engaging in something positive or creative like exercising, painting, writing, or anything else you love to do) to redirect the negative emotions and shift your energy, and being aware of other people's emotions, are all strategies you can use to connect and stay connected to source.

> "Feelings are really your GPS system for life. When you're supposed to do something, or not supposed to do something, your emotional guidance system lets you know."
>
> Oprah Winfrey

You also need to recognize that people act and make irrational or emotional decisions for logical reasons. In general, women make more emotional decisions for logical reasons than men when it comes to shopping, and men more than women when it comes to sports. A man, justifying the purchase of a Ferrari for investment purposes provides a good example. An example of the distaff side would be justifying the purchase of a $5,000 evening gown for $2,000 because it was a bargain at 60% off, it was the last one, and it could be handed down from generation to generation.

In fact, I am so sure that logical reasons are being used to justify emotional decisions that it became the inspiration for my retirement plan. When I am ready to retire, I'm going to rent a space on Fifth Avenue in New York City, the center of all marketplaces in the world, and nothing in my shop will have a sticker price of less than $20,000. The store will boast the latest in technology and be staffed with the most attractive salespeople you've ever seen. Sommeliers will describe the glasses of wine and champagne handed out to all customers upon entry (I'm still debating whether it will be by appointment only) while a caterer circles with well-paired hors d'oeuvres enabling the customers to eat while both shopping and mingling with guest celebrities. An interactive game here, a ball game on a flatscreen there. You know what? Just picture an adult version of Willy Wonka's Chocolate Factory.

> "People don't buy for logical reasons. They buy for emotional reasons."
>
> Zig Ziglar

I won't sell anything like jewelry upon which a real, hard or objective value could be placed. Instead, I'll sell unique, one-of-a-kind items that have subjective value only. I'll then advertise that I have the finest merchandise from all over the world and everything at the store will be 90% off. I guarantee that someone will be emotionally satisfied if they walk out of the store with a $30,000 ticketed item for $2,700 that I was able to buy in China for $100.

This irrationality is why I love working in sports and entertainment because it takes advantage of the emotional irrationality of baby boomers in America. It is the second best business to be in because someone will pay hundreds if not thousands of dollars for ink on a football, a picture, or a jersey. And, luckily for me and my business, this irrationality is shared across the socio-economic strata as typically prudent businessmen will pay an exorbitant amount of money for tickets, collectibles or the like. I say it's the second best business because there are other businesses that successfully trade off of the irrational part of the emotional relationship parents have to their children. For example, I know of parents who have gone hungry or moved so that their children can have private training lessons in various endeavors. I will not engage in a business built around selling hope to parents. In part, I won't because, most times, it's fueled by the parents' ego-driven thoughts on how great their child is that motivates the decisions. I also won't because of the pressure put on the child. I know that from my own experience. Because my parents thought more of me than I thought of myself when I was young, it put enormous pressure on me. I couldn't live up to the false expectations and values that my parents had placed on me. If anything, the want and desire must be the child's and it must be the

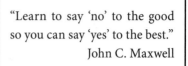

"Learn to say 'no' to the good so you can say 'yes' to the best."
John C. Maxwell

child's shared vision and manifestation with the parent, their own ego out of the way, merely providing the opportunity and empowerment.

Outside the realm of sports, entertainment, and businesses that prey upon parents' emotions, you still need to take caution. Eagles are able to tap in or align with your energy and emotions and will share a vision so you lose all sense of reality, objectivity, or true Penn Value. Half of your life will be spent selling, half buying. Again, if you can learn anything about buying, remember the extremely powerful word "No." But wait, didn't I earlier state that the universe does not know the word "No"? I did. "No" means "not at this time" because, in fact, the universe does only know "Yes" (as a matter of semantics, then, you could say that "No" actually means "Yes … I'm *not* interested in purchasing.")

You can always change the word "No" to "Yes", but the reverse is much more difficult. No matter how much you want something, remember, it is only an item and if someone else buys it, it was meant for them and not you. Learn to detach from your emotions and stay connected to source. You are better off going home, doing your due diligence to see where else you can buy it if it's something you really want. Let your emotions settle down, then go back the next day and say "Yes." Time is your ally. The more time you take, the better the attraction becomes and the more you will learn and allow yourself to attract what you truly need to be manifesting. Think about a time you bought something and got ripped off. Do you remember it? Did you ever not get something and regret it? What energy resonates greater with you now? The worst thing that can happen is that you buy it at the same price or it is gone. Either way, the best thing happened.

Ninety-nine percent of the time, something will change overnight. Either you won't want it anymore because all of the emotional feelings are gone, you found a better deal elsewhere – or, upon your return, you discover they've lowered the price. Only good things will happen from "No." Shift your mind and energy from thinking with scarcity, "What if it's sold?" to "Everything good happens if I wait." The universe is abundant and has enough of everything for everyone. Naturally, I'm referring to those items that you buy on emotion that can affect your finances and your life; this applies to large lifetime purchases, such as cars, expensive shoes, a large screen television. After all, a house is just a house. The people within the house are what make it a home. In fact, car dealers may not want to hear this, but if you want to buy a car, I'd highly recommend you renting it for a minimum of a weekend. In my opinion, it is well worth the money. Go out and find your car. Negotiate the price and then say "No." Rent the car for the weekend (Hertz, Avis, etc.), then make your decision. You'll get a lower price. You'll know what you're getting, and you'll get the emotions out of your system. If you allow all the emotional value to dissipate, you'll make a much more objective decision based on your Penn Value.

> "When dealing with people, let us remember we are not dealing with creatures of logic. We are dealing with creatures of emotion, creatures bustling with prejudices and motivated by pride and vanity."
>
> Dale Carnegie

Not all items that carry a lot of emotion and energy need be big ticket purchases. Food is a great example. Like money, food is a powerful energy and it carries tremendous emotional value. In fact, food may carry an even greater power than money because we need it for sustenance (money can buy you food, but in the end, if there was no money you could still survive so long as you had food). However, both have powerful energies and take on different meanings from individual to individual. In the same way, money may mean

> "Men decide far more problems by hate, love, lust, rage, sorrow, joy, hope, fear, illusion, or some other inward emotion, than by reality, authority, any legal standard, judicial precedent, or statute."
>
> Cicero

"freedom" to someone, food may mean "love". Therefore, like money, we need to be aware of the energy association so that we don't let our egos get in the way or corrode our connection to source and become self-destructive. Too much food is no better than too much money. And have you ever shopped for groceries when you were hungry? If so, can you point to one instance when you shopped when you were hungry that didn't end up in some sort of excessiveness? The point is, like everything else in life, there needs to be a balance between your emotions and your logic.

Strategy Principle – Key Element #4: Communication

As a teenager, you are sure about everything, but as you get older, you realize that you cannot be 100% sure – and that's fine! We also know how detrimental it is to carry the energy or need to be right. How many times have you thought you were 100% sure of something only to find out you were wrong? At least you don't have to suffer through my wife's "I told you so" dance! The bottom line in business is that everyone needs to be on the exact same page

> "The single biggest problem in communication is the illusion that it has taken place."
>
> George Bernard Shaw

(aligned) so there are no misunderstandings. Apples need to be compared to apples. The problem with words is that they have different meanings to different people and, even worse, they have different emotional associations. Question terminology that you may not be familiar with, or the context within which it is being used. Be more interested than interesting and learn to answer this situation with, "Let me check on that." Great questions are, "What did you mean by that?" or "What does that mean to you?"

I actually stress the need to "over-communicate". This ensures alignment, an easier energy flow, and in today's world, with so many means of communication, it's so simple to do. Yet, interestingly, even with more tools available to communicate, I've seen people communicating less, or should I say, they are communicating less effectively. As famed football coach and television analyst Lou Holtz says, "It doesn't matter what you said, it's what they heard." Don't be afraid to ask for clarification, confirm appointments/due dates/ receipts of emails or phone calls/facts/ and anything else that might result in misunderstandings or confusion later. With over-communication, we are living above the line in accountability and not in blame, shame and justification. With over-communication, we know how the ego works and we don't have a need to be right, a need to be offended or a need to be superior. When I'm aware that my communication is not being "heard", I create a strategy to change what I am saying and how I am saying it and see whether, statistically, more people now understand. I can impart what I think are great ideas all day long, but if I'm not reaching you, if I haven't communicated effectively, it doesn't matter what I'm saying. If I haven't been able to communicate effectively, I won't be able to share my vision to the

> "Years ago, I tried to top everybody, but I don't anymore, I realized it was killing conversation. When you're always trying for a topper you aren't really listening. It ruins communication."
>
> Groucho Marx

"nth" Power, to empower you so that you'll be able to teach someone else, or, at least shift your own energy to create more positive energy in the universe.

So, over-communicate by conversing effectively and never be afraid to ask for clarification. Warren Moon is a prime example of how to leverage the situational knowledge, experience and values of others, and excel by asking questions. His mom engrained the concept in him that if he didn't understand something, he should never be embarrassed to ask. Throughout his career, exposed to and surrounded by various experts in their field, Warren has made the most out of each stage of his life by asking questions of these influential, intelligent, and experienced individuals, and soaking up the information thereby provided to him. I know so many athletes similarly situated to Warren who failed because their egos had them act the fool. They cheated the system and never learned anything. Don't be afraid to tell someone that they are not communicating effectively. Do not let your ego get in the way. If you don't empower others by scaling your energy, then you only stay connected to source at an individual energy level, and in the end, you may as well stay home and work alone.

Communicating effectively with stable data also includes procedures, methodology and mechanisms in order for everyone to work, act and share within the same energy block and stay connected to source or goodness. In this way, if we over-communicate, we'll be able to keep the connection clean to both source and to each other. Then, rather than possible misalignment

> "Communication is the real work of leadership."
>
> Nitin Nohria

resulting from ineffective or under-communication, not only will we be able to manifest what we want individually, we'll also be able to create a collective belief and momentum which carries with it energy to the "nth" Power.

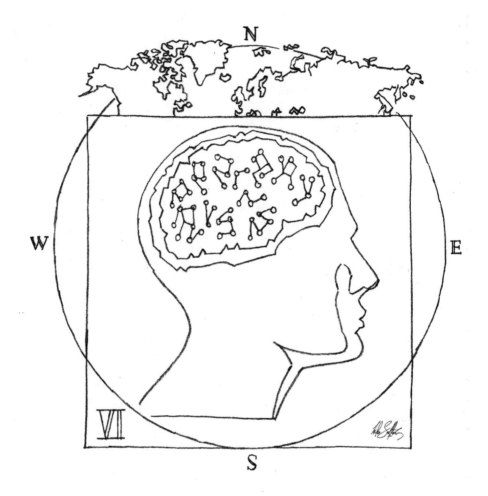

VI. PRINCIPLE SIX: UNDERSTANDING

"Any fool can know. The point is to understand."

Albert Einstein

You now have Foundation, Guideposts, Manifestation, Discipline, and the Strategy for putting these Principles in place. The next step is to manage, develop and understand all of these same Principles. The way we do this is by taking action, utilizing the energy correctly, and staying connected, as well as being aware when we're not connected. We, therefore, need to know, for instance, when we're feeling anxious instead of comfortable. We need to know whether or not we understand what we're looking at, or if we need to look at things differently. We need to know where the universe stands in order to see how much further it can be pushed without pushing too hard. Understanding is about recognizing the energy you've created through the other Principles, then utilizing and maximizing that energy to stay connected to source or goodness.

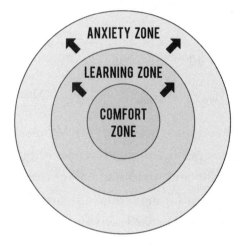

The comfort zone is that area that you know like back of your hand and takes no real thought on your part. It's an anxiety-free, warm and fuzzy place. I like to compare it to snuggling with your three-year-old at home on your couch. And, certainly, we all need to be in a place like that … occasionally. Just be careful not to extend your stay.

Just outside of the comfort zone sits the learning zone. You'll want to recognize the learning zone. This is where you want to live. It's not just learning in the educational sense, but it encompasses learning with regards to everything we do – from shooting baskets to communicating with others to meditation. Beyond the learning zone is the anxiety zone. It's just as important to know when we're

> "Move out of your comfort zone. You can only grow if you are willing to feel awkward and uncomfortable."
>
> Brian Tracy

stuck in the comfort zone and not challenging ourselves as it is to know when we're in the anxiety zone and pushing ourselves a little too hard. We do want to cross over into the anxiety zone, but shift our energy once we get there and take a little step back. If you stay out in the anxiety zone too far or too long, your comfort zone and learning zone will actually get smaller and you will be able to handle less and less.

Living in the anxiety zone can result in tunnel vision, nervous breakdowns, drug and alcohol abuse and the like. However, if you stay in the learning zone and keep "pushing out", eventually, everything you learned now becomes your comfort zone and what used to make you anxious is now your learning zone. Creating or changing effective habits will take you out of the comfort zone – however, the challenges and struggles that come with it are well worth it. If you can continuously self-identify these zones, you'll be amazed at what you can accomplish in all aspects of life. This is a great tool for self-actualization and connecting to source and goodness, thereby allowing you to stay fulfilled and inspired.

Golf is a good example. In my opinion as a well-known sports guy, golf is a skill, not a sport. This is not to say that some golfers, like Tiger Woods, aren't also great athletes, but he is a great athlete who has great skill in playing golf, and it would be no different than if he bowled, shot guns, or played darts. The interesting example of these "skill sports" is that in practicing over and over and committing yourself, you become

> "To the degree we're not living our dreams, our comfort zone has more control of us than we have over ourselves."
> Peter McWilliams

more comfortable with shots or throws that used to make you anxious, and you eventually become better at that skill.

The abstract for Malcolm Gladwell's book, *Outliers: The Story of Success*, proves enlightening:

> "In this stunning new book, Malcolm Gladwell takes us
> on an intellectual journey through the world of "outliers"
> – the best and the brightest, the most famous and the

most successful. He asks the question: what makes high-achievers different?

His answer is that we pay too much attention to what successful people are like, and too little attention to where they are from: that is, their culture, their family, their generation, and the idiosyncratic experiences of their upbringing. Along the way he explains the secrets of software billionaires, what it takes to be a great soccer player, why Asians are good at math, and what made the Beatles the greatest rock band. Early exposure and repetition."

This same philosophy holds true in life. Anything you like or love to do: practice. You'll feel good learning, you consistently push yourself to stay connected; and to be at peace and happiness and feeling good is, ultimately, what we all really want.

Understanding Principle – Key Element #2: The Press

Most of us are familiar with the "I Love Lucy" school of grape stomping, and I think I'd enjoy dancing around and crushing grapes barefoot in a wooden tub to the strains of Italian music. But the reality is that nowadays winemakers use presses to extract the juice from newly harvested grapes. There are a few different types of presses, but, essentially they all work the same way. Grapes are placed inside the press and some pressure is then added to get the juice out. When the flow of juice from the press slows or stops, more pressure is added. And yet more pressure is added again until, finally, no juice remains and all that you have left are spent skins, seeds and maybe some stems.

> "Negotiating techniques do not work all that well with kids, because in the middle of a negotiation, they will say something completely unrelated such as, 'You know what? I have a belly button!' and completely throw you off guard."
>
> Bo Bennett

While this analogy does leave me longing for a glass of wine, what we all need to do is press the grapes of life and the universe. Press the grapes, and if juice comes out, press it again and keep pressing until there is no more juice. If you don't think these are core energies of the universe, ask any parent with a four- or five-year-old – those kids know how to "press the grapes" better than anyone; they are both tireless and relentless.

In a business sense, this Key Element is a negotiation tool. If people you are negotiating with are willing to give, it is the natural flow and you shouldn't be afraid to receive, and you shouldn't be afraid to keep asking. Keep "pressing the grapes"; keep asking until they say "no" three times. Make sure that you have done everything you can to create the abundance that you're looking for by asking as many open- and closed-ended questions as you can. The open-ended questions allow you to understand the other party's perspective and their reasons and impacts, while the close-ended questions narrow down the other party's initial responses. This helps to become more aligned with the capabilities you possess (if successful, this is the point where I habitually present the summary as a strategy to overly and effectively communicate).

For example, I was negotiating an appearance by a Hall of Fame football player with a Fortune 500 CEO, who was a typical, irrational middle-aged man in love with his childhood idol. During negotiations, when I asked for a certain dollar amount ... he said "Yes." When I asked for a private jet ... he said "Yes." When I asked for the football player's assistant to come in addition to the player... he said "Yes." When I asked for a Presidential suite ... he said "Yes." I kept asking for more and more until he finally said "No" three times. He was so irrational that I probably could've gotten him to spring for the Hall of Famer's nanny's dog to come as well.

> "If women ran the world we wouldn't have wars, just intense negotiations every 28 days."
> Robin Williams

In life and in business, you will not receive if you don't ask or command the universe. And don't stop commanding or you will create resistance for yourself. Command means "work with" the universe; do not get it confused with Demand! This is not about trying to drain someone else of their energy, or wearing the other party down by pressing again and again (in that case, my analogy would have been a full-court "press" or even the White House "Press" Corps, who are relentless in their pursuit). This is all about making sure that you've done everything you can to find alignment and create the abundance you seek by staying connected and in the flow.

I once had an employee who wanted to go to a party at the Playboy mansion taking place the next week. I made a phone call on his behalf, and he went to the party. Six other employees came in after the party and wanted to know why they couldn't have gone to the Playboy mansion. My response was, "You didn't ask." If you don't ask, it is not out there in the universe in the first place; what you want is not just going to fall in your lap. Have confidence in yourself. Attract what you want by stimulating the universe and pressing the grapes.

And then, ask for even more. Another employee, Gus, who was purchasing shirts for us, was content that the shirt company had reduced the price $1 for him from $17 which was 80% off retail (the price we had previously paid) to a new price of $16. I

> "Negotiation in the classic diplomatic sense assumes parties more anxious to agree than to disagree."
> Dean Acheson

told Gus to ask the shirt company to reduce the price to $10. When Gus hesitated, I sarcastically asked him, "Do you work for me or them?" After Gus sheepishly exited my office, I picked up the phone and personally spoke to an executive at the shirt company. I told him I wanted the shirts for $10. Twice, he said "No, I can't do it," and each time I "walked" away. Then, on my third request, he finally agreed to $12.50 per shirt and this included our Sports1Marketing logo, which normally costs us an additional $2.50 per shirt.

The shirt company did not have to sell to us at my asking price. The legal expression "Caveat emptor" means "let the buyer beware." Nowhere does the law say "let the seller beware." As the seller, you set the value for your product and upon the sale, you receive exactly what you bargained for – my money. There is a bottom line Penn Value to everything in life and in business, and we need to "Press" to stay connected to goodness to maximize the source energy for all parties involved.

Especially in life, you must "Press" to take a stand on your personal beliefs. For years, I was someone who didn't stand up for my personal beliefs. I always wanted to be the diplomat. Trust me when I say that it's important to stand up for what you believe in and stay connected to source when something goes against your personal beliefs. Again, if you don't think this is a core energy of the universe, something that is not learned, how is it that a two-year-old can remain so persistent? "Eat your peas." "No!" "Eat your peas." "No!!" We lose this ability to connect to source and stand up for what we believe in. This happens over time through our socio-economic environment, our experience value, our insecurities, and all of the other energies we carry from this life, or even past lives (if this is something you believe in). After years of corroding my connection, I now stand up for my beliefs because I would rather be hated for who I am than loved for who I am not. But the bottom line is, if a two-year-old can stand up for him- or herself and what they believe in, you can too.

> "Friendship is constant in all other things
> Save in the office and affairs of love:
> Therefore all hearts in love use their own tongues;
> Let every eye negotiate for itself,
> And trust no agent."
>
> William Shakespeare

You need to understand the give and take of the universe. Based on the Principles in this book, you need to understand yourself. Then, to get the most out of life and business – to thoroughly press the grapes – all you really need to do is stay connected to source or goodness. If you understand this, you'll realize that it's not a matter of me out-negotiating you or you having to compromise your beliefs. All can enjoy in the abundance of the universe.

Understanding Principle – Key Element #3:
Shift The Paradigm

Quid pro quo is a Latin term that I learned in law school. It means if I give you something, you need to give me something back. This is carrying an energy of scarcity rather than looking at an abundant universe. I suggest trusting the universe and reversing this *quid pro quo* mentality. Shift the paradigm of giving ... *trust* the universe and just give with no scarcity apprehensions or energy, then be willing and prepared to receive. Think about it. It stems from the Reverse Ben Franklin Effect.

> "Let mortals beware of words
> For with words we lie
> Can speak peace
> When we mean war
> But song is true
> Let music for peace
> Be the paradigm
> For peace means change
> At the right time."
>
> W. H. Auden

Have you ever been in an abundant situation where you said to someone, "I'll do this for you" with no expectation, and then they suddenly said, "Hey, I have these two tickets. Would you like to come?" or something to the effect of what can they then do for you? As difficult as it might seem, think what would happen if you shifted the paradigm in, say, the context of a divorce. *Quid pro quo* would be "You can have joint custody of the kids, but you need to give me the house." Reverse *quid pro quo* would be "Let me know how I can work with you and give you the support you need, because in my opinion, it's better for our children to be with you since you're their mom, you're a tremendous mom, they love you and whatever you deem is best for our children is what I want." This changes the energy. I can now hear the mother saying, "I appreciate that. Why don't you take Tuesdays, Thursdays and Saturdays. And we can work together about scheduling vacations." Also, "How would you like to handle the house because I know that you put your heart and soul into building it?"

Try to give what resources and assets you can, be it in life or business, with no expectations of receiving. If you stay connected to source and goodness you will be abundant and receive abundance. I often get this opportunity on the phone; before asking for anything, I'll say, "I can get you *this*" or "let me send you *that*". If you have it, give first before you ask to take. Shifting the paradigm is reversing the tendency to see only what's clearly in front of you and thinking abundantly.

> "Your paradigm is so intrinsic to your mental process that you are hardly aware of its existence, until you try to communicate with someone with a different paradigm."
>
> Donella Meadows

Warren and I do a lot of work with St. Jude Research Hospital. One of the things that attracted me to St. Jude was the founder, Danny Thomas. The entertainer started St. Jude with the dream that no child should die of cancer. He began raising the money on airplane flights. He'd get on the microphone, introduce himself, then tell the passengers, "I'm trying to raise $1.2 million dollars with the goal of no more children dying of cancer, and I'd appreciate any donation." He'd then walk up and down the aisle holding out his hat. Later, he began reaching out to his entertainer friends. Before he started St. Jude, only 4% of children with leukemia survived. Today, that number is over 96%. Fair to say, Danny Thomas created a significant collective belief by, initially, walking up and down an aisle with his individual manifestation.

Danny Thomas is quoted as saying, "Those who take eat well at night, but those who give sleep well at night." To me, this encapsulates the concept of "Shifting the Paradigm" (as well as believing in yourself, trusting the universe, and staying connected to source and goodness). Danny broke away from the Rat Pack and the big, flashy

Hollywood stars of the `50s and `60s to use what source had given him to combat childhood cancer. The hospital also took on Danny's collective energy and belief. My favorite example of abundance is that St. Jude takes the results of its millions of research dollars and posts them immediately for all the other hospitals in the world to use to cure cancer. They do not need to be "the hospital that cured cancer." They are completely abundant and only want to see cancer cured regardless of who gets it done. There are many other examples of how abundant St. Jude Research hospital is, and how Danny Thomas' abundance was the spark to shift the paradigm of medical research to cure cancer. Danny Thomas trusted the universe that everything will happen in its time, and St. Jude is now the second largest charity in the world with donations approaching $1 billion dollars a year! How fitting that St. Jude is the Patron Saint of the Impossible.

> "The historian of science may be tempted to exclaim that when paradigms change, the world itself changes with them."
>
> Thomas Kuhn

Understanding Principle – Key Element #4: Maximize Momentum

I read an article in late September, but it could be any September of any year, discussing New Year's resolutions made, and encouraging people not to give up as they enter the fourth quarter, even if they haven't taken one step toward their goal or objective. The article challenged the reader to test themselves now and not to wait until next year. I wholeheartedly agree. Put a plan together today, maximize momentum, then implement a brand-new plan come next year. The point is you need to start *somewhere* – and when you do you'll be amazed at what you can achieve.

> "Getting momentum going is the most difficult part of the job, and often taking the first step is enough to prompt you to make the best of your day."
>
> Robert J. McKain

In general, a vision board is a great starting point. A vision board can take on many shapes, sizes or even platforms – you can create one on anything from a poster board to a cell phone to just visualizing it in your mind – but it usually contains an image or a collection of images or words describing things you want to attract into your life. It can be a picture of a dog you want, words indicating that you'd like to have more responsibility in your job, a visualization of how you'd like to be a kind, responsible person. I know someone who cut out and placed a picture of his "ideal" dream house on his vision board, and five years later he bought that exact house. This did not happen by accident! Vision boards are great vehicles for focusing your positive energy on what you'd like to manifest.

Once you make it, look at it daily, think about it and let your mental waves make whatever is there happen. The more you focus on it and think about it, the more it is drawn to you, thereby allowing you to achieve that goal. And if what you are intending to manifest has not arrived yet, don't think you're doing something wrong. Trust the universe and stay connected to source. If you think it … it will come.

Lists are another form of a vision board, and a great idea. I read a statistic that people who use lists are 25% more productive than people who don't. Given how we can only keep four to seven things in the forefront of our mind, it is well worth your time to make a list concerning what you are going to do for the day lest you forget anything. First, prioritize it, then check off items

> "The most important thing you can do to achieve your goals is to make sure that as soon as you set them, you immediately begin to create momentum."
>
> Anthony Robbins

upon accomplishing the task. Similarly, a vision board can be used as a list. Anything that can help you stay focused, connected, or remind you of what you need to do can act as and be considered a vision board, even a to-do list.

You now understand how to manifest your own vision or visions. In business, it's about shared visions. Sharing a vision is a process to ultimately reach an agreement or understanding where all involved see the vision as beneficial. It begins with stimulating an interest in others regarding you, your services and/or your company with the purpose of transitioning that energy into a shared vision. But first you need to define what their critical business issues are so you can help solve them. As discussed, you need to be very specific on what you want to stimulate or attract. For example, at Sports 1 Marketing, our employees make phone calls to generate curiosity about what we do, or can offer. This is their clearly defined objective. If they call and reach a voicemail, their sole objective becomes getting the person to call them back. If someone does answer, their sole objective becomes calendaring a time for me to speak to that individual.

With this simple process, how do they generate curiosity? They briefly explain who we are and inform them why we are calling.

"What project?" "Are you looking for a donation?" are responses the employees typically receive. They reply, "I don't know? All I've been asked to do is to set up a call for my boss, David Meltzer (and/or Warren Moon). Are you available at 10 a.m. tomorrow?" This is a simple example of generating curiosity with a clearly defined objective. The curiosity is "What the hell does Dave Meltzer and Warren Moon want with me and my product?" And the clearly defined objective is to get them to say: "Sure, why not? Put me down for 10 a.m."

Everyone can come up with some way to create curiosity about who they are and what they can do if they're aligned to

> "Success requires first expending ten units of effort to produce one unit of results. Your momentum will then produce ten units of results with each unit of effort."
> Charles J. Givens

the right audience via Principle V – Strategy. Don't go on to any other steps before you've created curiosity. If you get an answering machine, don't over-educate or attempt to sell. If you go beyond your sole objective, you are attempting to create a vision too early. You are setting yourself up for resistance, rejection, or having to reengineer the vision.

Once you've generated the curiosity and are communicating with the other party, you then proceed to defining critical business issues for them. These are issues you know the customer or prospective customer has, but that he/she doesn't want to admit, or ones that don't appear on the surface. Examples of this would be the customer doesn't have readily available money, the customer has excess inventory, or the customer's business is down 28%. But it's akin to someone who drinks too much – they can't identify the problem on their own, can't get out of their own way, and can't get past their own deniability. Part of the transition is getting the customer to become aware of, and admit to, this need or deficiency, because you can't tell the customer that he or she needs this. To accomplish this, you need to first ask the before-described open-ended, non-leading questions; in this case, geared toward making them comfortable, so they'll provide their own positive energy to talk about what's going on: "Have you ever thought about x, y or z?" Then you move on to before-described closed-ended or leading questions designed to drive them to exactly what you can provide, such as, "I work with many companies like yours and it helped their bottom line when I was able to do x, y and z. Would that be of interest to you?"

> "Commitment is the ignitor of momentum."
>
> Peg Wood

Utilize open- and closed-ended questions to explore the reasons they should do it, and the impact it will have on their business. Tie this in to the capabilities you have, or some past performance on your part, and you'll get them to extract, expose and admit their critical business issues. In the end, it needs to be *their* reasons, impact, and capabilities from their ideas. The Penn Value needs to be clearly seen by all. You want to demonstrate the value you'll be providing in relation to the customer's personal values, experience values, giving and receiving values as discussed under Principle I, Foundation. The prospect must feel that they're getting the best deal. Everyone needs to see this as a "win-win" situation.

But how do you find out the customer's personal, experience, giving and receiving values so that you can address them? The answer is through the exact same process that you used to get them to admit their critical business issues. You ask them questions. Again, start with open-ended questions to delve into their personal, experience, giving and receiving values. "What do you like about it?" "What do you like to do?" "Have you always been in this field?" Then begin the close-ended follow-up questions to narrow down the reasons and impacts aligned with your capabilities in order to share a vision. "Did that work for you?" "Did you like that part of it?"

This process of sharing a vision assessment helps create the answer you want. The customer will want to proceed because, and excuse the double negative, there are no reasons not to move forward with you. You'll be providing value, items, benefits, or features that relate to how much money they want to make, how many people they can help, how much of a great experience they'll enjoy (which provides intangible value), all the while affecting their personal values. You've taken into account and used all the Principles, have trusted the universe and connected to source, and have made adjustments so that you are now aligned with the customer, having found the point that makes everyone happy.

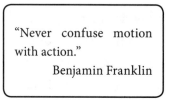

"Never confuse motion with action."

Benjamin Franklin

The next step is to transition that business vision. You need the customer to articulate to you a clear summary of your agreement. "Would it be fair to say, in summary, that this is what we talked about … that this is the value that it has, and do you see any reason why you wouldn't want to move forward?" This leads to the creation of a final agreement which everyone signs. This agreement is purportedly the articulation and memorialization of a meeting of the minds. Make sure it is in writing, signed and dated. If you're afraid of offending someone by asking them to put it in writing, tell them it is not so much about trust as it's about making sure you remember everything that was discussed, and this is the best way to ensure your intent to get them everything that you are promising.

On my first day of my criminal law class in law school, a student barged into the room and started screaming at the professor about a bad grade he'd received from the prior semester. The student then punched the professor, knocking him to the floor, before running out of the room. We were stunned, wide-eyed and open-mouthed, frozen in our seats. We had no idea that the professor faked the whole episode until he jumped to his feet and began asking us questions geared toward describing the assailant. People had widely different recollections as to everything from height to hair color to clothing.

I've also seen "The Invisible Gorilla" video, the selective attention test by Dr. Daniel Simons, Professor in the Department of Psychology and the Beckman Institute at the University of Illinois, where three people in white shirts and three in black shirts are bouncing basketballs and passing them back and forth. Those viewing this video are supposed to take note of how many times these players pass the ball either by bounce or in the air. Not only do viewers get the number wrong, but when first shown at Harvard University only 50% watching saw someone dressed in a gorilla costume slowly and

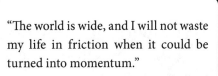

"The world is wide, and I will not waste my life in friction when it could be turned into momentum."

Frances Willard

quite clearly walk into the frame, pound his chest three times, then walk slowly off the screen.

The point is that while we can trust the universe, we can't always trust our senses, especially our memories. Make absolutely sure that the agreed upon terms and obligations are clearly spelled out in writing. As the old saying goes, "The faintest ink is better than the brightest memory". Feign a poor memory if you have to, but getting the agreement in writing is vital. The agreement is the embodiment of alignment –with your customer, with you, with your own people – and the process will expose, prior to signature, any places where there is misalignment.

Next, put together a success criteria. Here's an example of one:

SUCCESS CRITERIA

ORIGINAL CONTENT

1. Ford Gum will have full rights to repurpose and use the "A Never Was Been" content showcasing Big League Chew in any/all marketing efforts online, in social media, and on the company website.

MET EXPECTATIONS □   EXCEEDED EXPECTATIONS □

NATIONWIDE DISTRIBUTION

2. "A Never Was Been" will premiere in November and be available for viewing nationwide until late February during the New Hollywood (NUHO) Film Festival where the film and Big League Chew will be showcased to over 2,000,000 people from around the country.

MET EXPECTATIONS □   EXCEEDED EXPECTATIONS □

PUBLICITY & EXPOSURE

3. Big League Chew brand logo will be included in a full page "A Never Was Been" advertisement showcased on the front inside cover of the November/December issue of Baseball Digest (330,000+ subscribers).

MET EXPECTATIONS □   EXCEEDED EXPECTATIONS □

4. Product Integration of Big League Chew throughout Sports Documentary "A Never Was Been".

MET EXPECTATIONS □   EXCEEDED EXPECTATIONS □

5. Big League Chew shown being chewed by main character Sean Pamphilon during "A Never Was Been".

MET EXPECTATIONS ☐   EXCEEDED EXPECTATIONS ☐

6. Big League Chew shown being chewed by supporting characters in the film.

MET EXPECTATIONS ☐   EXCEEDED EXPECTATIONS ☐

7. Big League Chew shown being chewed by spectators.

MET EXPECTATIONS ☐   EXCEEDED EXPECTATIONS ☐

8. Verbal mentions of Big League Chew by players during the film.

MET EXPECTATIONS ☐   EXCEEDED EXPECTATIONS ☐

9. Post Production recap with photos from event.

MET EXPECTATIONS ☐   EXCEEDED EXPECTATIONS ☐

EXCLUSIVITY

10. Category Exclusivity for Big League Chew (Chewing Gum) in Sports Documentary "A Never Was Been".

MET EXPECTATIONS ☐   EXCEEDED EXPECTATIONS ☐

BRANDING

11. Big League Chew branding, banners, signage, logos, etc. displayed in/around the baseball field where filming will take place to create brand awareness, publicity, and exposure.

MET EXPECTATIONS ☐   EXCEEDED EXPECTATIONS ☐

12. Brand Association and Endorsement by Warren Moon and Sports 1 Marketing.

MET EXPECTATIONS ☐   EXCEEDED EXPECTATIONS ☐

This is the business equivalent of a vision board, or better yet, it's a "shared vision board". It is part of the shared vision. It lays out in measurable terms what must be done for the project to be acceptable to the client stakeholders and end users who will be effected by the project. Otherwise, if you don't get to the purpose of the project, you'll never get to the Penn Value.

> "It is not of importance where we stand, but in what direction we are moving."
>
> Unknown Author

List out the specifics of what exactly, and in what time frame, things will be aligned with the successes that you want. List out the vision and the resources necessary to implement it. Again, utilize what works best for you – a true vision board, a "to do" list, a computer application, a drawing – and, you can be like me and also meditate on it. But if you're not thinking about it, how are you ever going to get there ... or, as will be expanded upon, how can you exceed a clients' expectations?

Think of the success criteria like the agenda you create before you go on a trip. You have names, phone numbers, addresses, reservations, confirmation numbers, directions, tickets, times, schedules, and you've left your contact information with a friend or relative. This creates the subtleties of success. If you've really thought through all of the details prior to leaving, the actual trip becomes the easy part. And, with all bases covered, the relaxing part. The implementation of the success criteria is your trip. It takes energy, but it is fun and fulfilling. As you list out the specifics, ensure that all of the things in the success criteria are measureable and can be checked off. Make sure that each individual item is realistic; it won't do you any good to list things in your success criteria that you can't perform. Be aware of conflict within your success criteria. For example, the promise of high quality, early delivery and low cost as a group may have conflicting goals and, thus, be unrealistic. Ask yourself whether your success criteria forms a

> "Sometimes being pushed to the wall gives you the momentum necessary to get over it!"
>
> Peter de Jager

complete list of criteria to define an outcome that is acceptable to your customer as part of the shared vision. Have you included a "purpose" checklist – the personal level required to use, operate or deliver? Does it include performance levels, accuracy, availability, reliability, mean and maximum time to repair or fix, developmental costs, running costs, security, ease of use, timing and the like? It can include things like the client satisfaction as far as a product or a service, accessibility, training, additional business from client ... or, it can be as simple as three things. But write them down.

Once you have your success criteria, review and confirm it with your client. For example, Sports 1 Marketing was involved in a baseball deal. Our success criteria clearly told those clients involved that they'd be getting three very specific things: their logo on the inside cover of a major baseball publication; content that they could repurpose for their use; and their logo front and center in the film to be featured at the film festival. And, in return, the clients were clearly made aware of *what* they needed to do: supply their logo, their product, and full payment – and *when* each of these obligations on their part was due. If the success criteria is for an event, go over it personally with your client before, during, and after the event.

The implementation of the success criteria is where everything comes together. You need to be smart and creative. You need to keep in mind external or extraneous things you can do for your customer to exceed expectations – such as in the case of my business, can I bring them a Sports 1 Marketing shirt that they'd like ... or a Warren Moon autographed picture? They will attach the emotions of the experience of Sports 1 Marketing exceeding their expectations to what they received, including our brand and presence. In the case of your business, can you put a thank-you card in the mail, or send a little gift? Like the act of

> "One way to keep momentum going is to have constantly greater goals."
>
> Michael Korda

filling up the car for your spouse or partner, these things usually take only minutes, but it's that little bit extra that leads to success. These are the things that will be remembered and go a long way. Above all, you need to stay connected to source or goodness.

Schedule the implementation like you would schedule anything else. Make sure a logistical analysis has taken place. Are any other resources going to be needed, such as legal, partners, technical or administrative? The what, who, how, where and when is going to be utilized and necessary to successfully move forward, and confirmation of these by the client only adds to the appearance of your professionalism.

The success criteria, with the promises, expectations, vision, and resources all laid out, will be the final grade on how you get something to thrive. If you meet the success criteria standards, the client will judge the agreed-upon relationship successful. For example, we had one client who only wanted to make sure that they had their picture taken with famous athletes, and we made the arrangements. We had another client who was more interested in social networking, so Warren and six of our clients tweeted on this other client's behalf. Yet another client was solely interested in knowing that his product and signage were at the event. Another simply wanted to sample tequila and cigars at an event. These one or two measurable items, these critical performance indicators, provided the projects with objective criteria against which success could be measured.

> "When you're that successful, things have a momentum, and at a certain point you can't really tell whether you have created the momentum or it's creating you."
>
> Annie Lennox

And, yes, meeting all of the standards and connecting to goodness by *exceeding* expectations will guarantee success. But I urge you to exceed the success criteria and shared vision standards, thereby exceeding the client's expectations. This is the way to take your business to the "nth" Power. This guarantees that your customer will be automatic for continued or repeat business; and next time you won't need all of the time it initially took in developing or addressing all of the concerns. A simple phone call should now suffice when an opportunity or the like presents itself, *especially* when you've exceeded expectations.

In addition, a satisfied customer whose expectations have been exceeded will talk or has talked to others on your behalf. I've heard from people who had heard about events from others who want to make sure they can participate next year. I've also heard from new clients who have heard from others about us and now want to get involved with us. Without any exposing of any new opportunity, you're already at a stage of sharing a vision with this new individual. The clients whose expectations have been exceeded are also easy to approach to ask if there's anyone they might know who'd be interested in you and your services or product. Without hesitation, you'll be able to ask these clients questions to better understand their relationship capital and situational knowledge in order to leverage it. Or use the Ben Franklin effect and ask how you can help them, which, in turn, will then lead them to articulate how they can help you. Obviously it depends on your business, but with a great relationship, you may be able to even offer this client a channel partnership agreement, thereby incentivizing them to go out and help leverage opportunities for you. I promise you that the more you know about your client and exceed their expectations, the greater the number of opportunities that you'll be able to leverage and move your business towards the "nth" Power. You *will* be maximizing momentum.

> "The BIG push means being able to develop and sustain momentum toward your goal; it is the process of actively replacing excuses with winning habits, the ultimate excuses blockers. Moreover, it is being willing to go to the wall for what you want or believe in, to push beyond your previous mental and physical limits, no matter what it takes."
>
> Lorii Myers

Let me put this in terms of the 80/20/80 Rule. Most people believe they're completely finished with a transaction after they've shared the vision and entered into an agreement. As we discussed, 80% of the work is to stimulate the universe by spending more time planning, but you are actually only 20% done ... you're not even close to completion! Eighty percent of your effort is still needed in order to thrive, to create a legacy, to empower others after you've created a vision. Eighty percent of your time needs to be infusing the energy to manage and develop that vision.

80% STIMULATE INTEREST / **20**% AGREEMENT OF SHARED INTEREST / **80**% MANAGE AND DEVELOP VISION

This is what will eventually get you to the "nth" Power. You want to maximize the momentum when you are connected to goodness. Do this and I promise you, in business and life, you will attract exactly what you want and help others attract, as a collective belief or a shared vision, the abundance of making a lot of money, helping a lot of people, and having a lot of fun. The laws of our abundant universe have no choice but to attract everything you desire more accurately and rapidly.

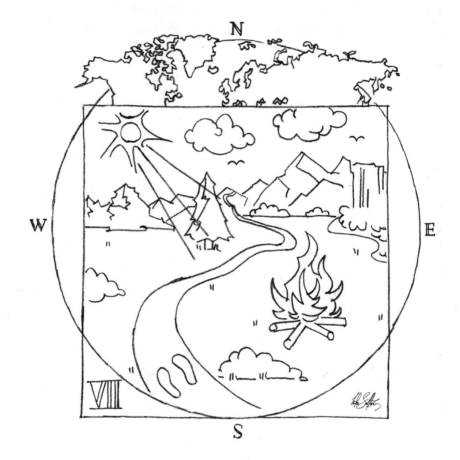

VII. PRINCIPLE SEVEN: DESTINATION

"All the world's a stage,
And all the men and women merely players;"

William Shakespeare

With these Principles, you now have the tools, strategy and understanding to manifest whatever you'd like both in life and business. This section is about the different directions or paths that I've observed in life and business that you, as an individual, can take. I'd analogize it to the "Force" in the *Star Wars* movies, a power that can be used for good or evil. You can take these Principles that you now have at your disposal, keep connected to source, and achieve the "nth" Power; or you have the choice to stagnate or even self-destruct. The role you want to play and, ultimately, your destination is completely up to you. I'd like to thank Lee Brower, who I spoke of in Section One, for providing me with the foundation – his "stages of empowerment" – for this Principle. This end result – this road map to each own's destination –is based on my observational directions.

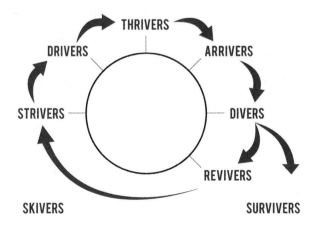

DESTINATION PRINCIPLE – KEY ELEMENT #1: STRIVE

Our objective is to become empowered and empower others to manifest what we want for ourselves as well as creating a shared vision to manifest good collectively. The first positive, productive step in that direction is to be a Striver. I say the "first positive, productive step" because there is an entitled stage of "going nowhere" that exists – the Skivers.

> "Authentic empowerment is the knowing that you are on purpose, doing God's work, peacefully and harmoniously."
> Wayne Dyer

Skivers (n): Scottish slang for lazy persons, people who don't pull their weight. In the States, we know them as "couch potatoes".

These are the people who cruise in life, the seemingly "entitled", who think they're deserving of something without having to put forth any effort. They live at home with their parents, or in a residence paid for by their parents, and never end up with a real job. Basically, they've been given everything they want without a mechanism to get it themselves.

I was jealous, puzzled, and offended by this type of person when I was growing up. I'd see these entitled Skivers, who were born on third base and thought they'd hit the home run, and I'd be so pissed off at them; but now I pray for their happiness. I now understand how lucky I was that my mother empowered me. For instance, there's a big difference between an entitlement, giving "Yes", and an empowerment, teaching "Yes". When your teenager approaches you and says, "Daddy, I want a car", what do you do? You could flatly say "No", thereby creating negative energies and not teach them empowerment, nor give them the benefit of the journey. You could rush out and buy them a car, spoiling them, and sending them driving down the road to entitlement where they'll learn nothing productive. Or you could say, "Terrific. Let's make a plan and figure out how we're going to get you a car."

The Skiver has no perspective on how to be empowered, nor how long and how much time it takes in order to manifest or attract. Their parents have actually condemned their own child; much like a man who has cut a butterfly's cocoon prematurely; without developed muscles from the challenge of breaking free from the cocoon, the butterfly will be unable to take flight and can't survive on its own … neither can the child.

> "If you have a comfortable life then you're going to become a nice sort of couch potato, and just take it in and be brain dead."
>
> Eric Khoo

If you don't want to raise a Skiver, don't do for them what they can do for themselves. You are cheating them. You are cutting the cocoon too early. It's like someone lifting in a weight room. If they need a spotter to get in one more rep, or add another five pounds of weight, give them a spot or add the weight. But don't lift the bar for them and say, "Congratulations, you did it!!" Similarly, don't throw the weights onto them and expect them to do it all by themselves. Appreciate the person, appreciate the thing, appreciate the situation, and add value to it.

If you, yourself, however, want to avoid being a Skiver altogether, or to pull yourself off of that proverbial couch and get a (meaningful) life, chose to get on the path and begin to be a Striver. This is the early, developmental stage of empowerment. This is the proverbial first step, striving to be what you want to be, a blend of empowered and entitled. Strivers want to actually achieve things and work hard, but they don't have clarity, balance, focus and a vision of where they want to go. The inability to attract with confidence is often attributable to a lack of appreciation of experience values. Strivers dream but have no focus.

Many people are Strivers, but are not willing to break through! They are like the piece of grass, growing in the dark, moist, soft and comfortable dirt underground, that won't break through the sun-soaked surface because it's too hard.

Every successful entrepreneur I've ever met is a breakthrough person. Everyone one of them has their own "breakthrough" story of how they were down to their last penny when … ! For those Strivers looking to break through, I offer my favorite poem:

> "Strive for excellence, not perfection."
> H. Jackson Brown Jr.

Don't Quit

When things go wrong, as they sometimes will,
When the road you're trudging seems all uphill,
When the funds are low and the debts are high,
And you want to smile, but you have to sigh,
When care is pressing you down a bit,
Rest, if you must, but don't you quit.

Life is queer with its twists and turns,
As every one of us sometimes learns,
And many a failure turns about,
When he might have won had he stuck it out;
Don't give up though the pace seems slow–
You may succeed with another blow.

Often the goal is nearer than
It seems to a faint and faltering man,
Often the struggler has given up,
When he might have captured the victor's cup,
And he learned too late when the night slipped down,
How close he was to the golden crown.
Success is failure turned inside out–

The silver tint of the clouds of doubt,
And you never can tell how close you are,
It may be near when it seems so far,
So stick to the fight when you're hardest hit–
It's when things seem worst that you mustn't quit.

- Author unknown

As we advance closer to our ultimate destination or objective, we next find "The Drivers". In this capacity, not only are you striving to do something, you are driving and aligning with others to help in propelling forward toward the Thrivers. Drivers are more empowered and less entitled. They are focused on and have started to

> "Be of service. Whether you make yourself available to a friend or co-worker, or you make time every month to do volunteer work, there is nothing that harvests more of a feeling of empowerment than being of service to someone in need."
>
> Gillian Anderson

manifest their vision, but have not put in all of the energy yet with regards to managing or developing that vision. While they are inspired and have, in fact, begun to attract what they desire, they have not yet empowered others. At the point where they do successfully stimulate others, that's when they are no longer "Drivers", but "Thrivers".

Steve Jobs built Apple around his own beliefs; then he was scrutinized, and was fired by his board of directors in 1985. Yet, he kept believing and stayed focused and connected, and upon being rehired in 1996, he, first a "Driver" (he was not stimulating others which led to his initial firing) then transitioning to a "Thriver", turned the company around with Apple becoming renowned as the leading music, movie, hardware and software company worldwide, and now providing .5% of our entire GNP.

The same holds true for billionaire Leslie Buckley, who founded Eircom International, a fixed, mobile and broadband telecommunications company. Leslie used his last $80,000 to make payroll. His determination to launch his network resulted in his connection to source, leading to the brilliant idea of providing free service to emergency service providers in exchange for using the roofs of their fire and police stations to put access points on to complete his network. This was his breakthrough, his "Driving" period, the beginning of his execution before he successfully moved on to the next stage where not only did he and his company become successful financially, but he created a free public service enabling police and fire personnel to better respond to emergencies. He could have disconnected from his beliefs, become scarce, shut down the company and lived off of his last $80,000.00, but he never would have thrived.

> "Continually strive to improve yourself."
> Anthony J. D'Angelo

If you stick to the seven Principles and the Key Elements, you will be able to maintain this connection to source or goodness and reach the ultimate stage where "The Thrivers" live. The Thrivers are absolutely empowered and have empowered everyone around them to "nth" Power. They not only manifest what they want, but they help others manifest as well. Their beliefs, energy and thoughts are now being put out there by others whom they helped and taught; and those beliefs, energies and thoughts become pervasive. In this stage, everyone involved is thriving and everything is growing exponentially because everyone's energy is being put forward and is aligned, and a global manifestation can occur. Here, you can live life in complete confidence without fear of failure because even if you lose it all, you know how to get it all back. This is the stage you want to remain in. Great men like Walt Disney, Carl Fisher and Albert Einstein are perfect examples of Thrivers.

> "If human beings are perceived as potentials rather than problems, as possessing strengths instead of weaknesses, as unlimited rather that dull and unresponsive, then they thrive and grow to their capabilities."
>
> Bob Conklin

Briefly, Walt Disney went bankrupt once and had failure after failure until he pushed the envelope by synchronizing sound to cartoon with *Steamboat Willie*. At one point, on the verge of a bankruptcy, he actually came home to tell his wife not to worry because he was going to build a kingdom about a mouse.

Carl Fisher, owner of the first car dealership in the U.S., founder of the Indianapolis 500, and the Lincoln and Holland Highways that connected the U.S. prior to the Eisenhower Interstate System, and the developer of Miami Beach, became the richest man on earth three different times … and was bankrupt in between. He also had to fight to get the first 500 run after he used the wrong surface material resulting in the deaths of drivers and spectators during initial races at the new Indianapolis Speedway.

Albert Einstein was expelled from school, could not hold a job, was ostracized by his family and the physics community. Yet, he went on to develop the Theory of Relativity, was instrumental in establishing quantum physics, and won the Nobel Prize.

> "In this life we get only those things for which we hunt, for which we strive, and for which we are willing to sacrifice."
>
> George Matthew Adams

These individuals all trusted the universe and connected to source. All of them are ICONS in their respective industries. All of them created a collective belief or energy that survived their existence on this planet. Despite all of their immense failures, they eventually triumphed and created legendary legacies.

As an aside, these men are also great examples of individuals who were not defined by what others said about them. Many myths and much innuendo swirled around these people. Yet, if you research the facts, you'll find that they were even more remarkable than you may have first believed. For instance, I'd heard that Einstein had failed math in elementary school. Who knows how the "overlooked genius" rumor started, but, in fact, Einstein had mastered differential and integral calculus before he was 15 years old (and yes, it is equally true that Israeli Prime Minister David Ben-Gurion approached Einstein in 1952 and offered him the position of President of Israel). This is even more reason not to let your ego define who you are based on what other people think of you, as discussed in Effective Habits, because misinformation is out there, especially with the prevalence of the Internet. I believe these individuals thrived because they stayed steadfastly connected and focused and used their energy productively.

Reaching Revive is a step process. Unfortunately, after people achieve the empowered utopia of Thriving, most newcomers start on the downward slope toward a lesser stage of empowerment known as "The Arrivers". This stage is where a person becomes self-entitled, which is different from the cruising Skiver, who were born or raised entitled. Arrivers

> "Power can be taken, but not given. The process of the taking is empowerment in itself."
>
> Gloria Steinem

have a need to be right, they possess a need to be offended. Basically, they get in their own way, have scarcity consciousness, and are disconnected from their goodness. They have a need to be superior, where being a better person is less important than being better than you. I know this type of person because it once described me to a "T". I had accomplished more than I ever dreamed of or thought possible. I outwardly projected a large ego that needed feeding to mask an energy that I was not worthy of all that I had done. I was no longer connected to source and lived in blame, shame and justification. I was empty, and, for the first time in my life, I was unhappy. I became self-absorbed and started attracting the wrong people and things into my life. I was self-entitled and wound up paying the price because if you stay an Arriver too long you, you soon become a Diver, as will be discussed shortly.

In fact, being an Arriver is far worse than being a Skiver because Arrivers ought to know better. Having gone through the process of striving and thriving, they possess an energy of self-importance. They break all of the rules on wanting or needing to be right, needing to feel superior, needing to have accolades and the like. They believe that their accolades and achievements signify who and what they are, and do not understand that there is always so much more to do.

They are clueless about or lose sight of their personal, experience, giving or receiving values. They become empty as their egos become bloated. Arrivers not only start to self-sabotage and drain energy from themselves, they also lose appreciation and begin to attract "like kinds" or like-minded people who carry the same self-absorbed and self-destructive energy. They stop being able to help and empower, and start entitling others.

How do you recognize an Arriver? Be aware of your and other's thoughts and words around you ..."I am the greatest athlete of all time." "I own a Ferrari." "Don't you know who I am???" These statements are all about "I" and the Ego. When you start thinking these types of statements, you are completely disconnected and need to adjust and "Cancel" those vibrations.

Ultimately, I continued on to the next downward stage of empowerment, "The Divers". Most Arrivers fall to this stage and, believe me, this is not a direction that you want to be heading. In our society, this usually manifests itself as drug and alcohol use, or other self-destructive behavior. Divers usually start losing everything, both consciously and unconsciously. All relationships, finances, experiences and the like fall to the wayside. They look for and attract all of the wrong things.

Unless they choose to no longer remain on this plane, Divers have two directions they can go. They can either become Survivors or Revivers. Survivors are those people who accept their

> 'There are always survivors at a massacre. Among the victors, if nowhere else."
>
> Lois McMaster Bujold

circumstances and have no motivation to become Revivers. They have flat-lined like Skivers. This is not to say that they can't at some point become "enlightened" or "empowered" and decide to become Revivers, in the same way a Skiver could decide to get off the couch, turn off the television, and become a Striver.

Revivers are the ones who pick themselves up, dust themselves off, and get back into the proverbial game, both in life and business. They reenter as a Driver or a Striver, rarely a Thriver, because it generally takes some time to get restarted and climb back up and clean the connection to goodness. That said, Revivers still typically take less time to make it back to becoming Thrivers than say a first time Striver or even a Driver, as they are fully aware of what it took to get there before – they have the situational knowledge and a better foundation through the lessons of their destiny – and once again inspired or empowered, know that things don't happen overnight, and they just need some time to get their act back together. Revivers know how to connect to

> "Any great work of art … revives and readapts time and space, and the measure of its success is the extent to which it makes you an inhabitant of that world – the extent to which it invites you in and lets you breathe its strange, special air."
>
> Leonard Bernstein

source or goodness, so it doesn't take much time to start recreating or manifesting again what they desire. They also know how to inspire and empower others to create collective energies and beliefs and attract with accuracy and confidence. This is why the "comeback stories" are the most attractive stories in our society … "Everybody loves a comeback!"

In fact, "Everybody loves a comeback" is what Leigh Steinberg used to tell his client athletes whenever they would screw up; and Leigh Steinberg himself is a classic example of a Reviver – of a great comeback story – who I could not be more proud of. As quoted in *USA Today*, Leigh said:

> "The American people relish the fall of the high and mighty. People get away from their own troubles by escaping into a celebrity driven press where they can feel better about themselves from the failures of others. … But

people also love the comeback story because they feel that everyone will experience adversity and want the potential for rebirth and revival."

A brilliant man, Leigh, again is widely regarded as the first of the super sports agents. Anyway, Leigh battled alcoholism for twenty years and lost almost everything he had to the disease, including his life. At the age of 65, he could have remained a Survivor ... or worse. Instead, he became and has remained sober and is now teaching Sports Law at Chapman University's School of Law, is back to being a certified agent, published a book, and has a newly funded company. Again, I cannot begin to tell you how much I respect my friend and mentor Leigh for becoming a Reviver!

> "Sometimes you hit a point where you either change or self-destruct."
>
> Sam Stevens

The concept of like attracting likes is probably, as you've read, what attracted me to Leigh in the first place. Unfortunately, I quickly became an Arriver, then went on my own downward spiral at one stage in my life. As I've said, being an Arriver is just as dangerous as being born a Skiver, or, perhaps, even worse because the fall is greater and you know where you've been and all it took to get there. It's no fun to become self-entitled and self-destructive. I felt that I wasn't worthy of my state of thriving and everything that I'd achieved. Again, in life and business, this is precipitated by things such as spending an excessive amount of money, not being in balance with and living within all of your Principles and Key Elements. Effective habits change for the worse. Bad habits have their cumulative effect. Instant gratification takes hold. At some point, the blame, shame and justification begins. You start telling yourself, "This can't be me. I'm successful. I'm a thriver. It must be everyone around me."

Be aware of these stages of empowerment and the vicious cycle that exists. Make sure you don't become an Arriver, then a Diver – but if you do, make certain you become a Reviver and not a Survivor. Striving then Driving followed by Thriving is the road to fulfillment and your peaceful destination of staying connected to goodness. If you use your free will to get connected and stay connected to goodness or source, you'll not run any risk of being an Arriver or Diver. So keep pushing forward when obstacles inevitably pop up along the way because, really, isn't life all about perspective, and aren't obstacles merely opportunities for personal growth and experience?

In fact, when I went through my transformation and enlightenment, I decided that I needed reminders of my Seven Principles and the Keys to staying connected. One of those reminders was Teddy Roosevelt's aforementioned book, *The Strenuous Life*, which, to this day, I keep on my bathroom sink next to my toothbrush. Thought to epitomize his beliefs, both personally and politically, the book does more than simply articulate the value of the journey and experiences gained. It praises or finds valuable those journeys or lives that are difficult because those are the journeys or lives that we truly learn from and make us stronger. As it states, "It is hard to fail, but it is worse to never to have tried to succeed." Additionally, the book criticizes those who choose journeys or lives filled with ease, "A mere life of ease is not in the end a very satisfactory life, and, above all, it is a life which ultimately unfits those who follow it for serious work in the world."

> "Be the flame, not the moth."
> Giacomo Casanova

I've laid out the Principle paths, but the choice is now yours. Get Connected, Remain Connected, and Stay Thriving, My Friends.

CONCLUSION

Perhaps after reading this book, you still have some doubt? Well, what do you think a guy a hundred years ago would have said if I'd told him he'd be able to talk to and see someone on the other side of the world on a device made of aluminum, plastic, and glass that he could hold in his hand? You have the free will to choose to follow what you've read or not, but I think once you start, you'll believe, and be inspired to continue wholeheartedly.

I strive to follow every day what I've laid out in this book. Have I successfully achieved all of these things? Absolutely not. Does that make me a hypocritic? No. I don't think I'd be on this plane if I could perform at the level of my knowledge of what I believe to be true. I believe that when you reach a certain point of enlightenment, you vibrate so fast that you don't want to stay on this plane, and that there are better places for you to be. The bottom line is that I'm still here, so I must have some more learning to do; and the fact that I'm still here reminds me to do a quick run-through of all of the Principles and Key Elements on my vision board, lists, diagrams or whatever I am using as my tool every day when I meditate.

When meditating, after I've increased my vibration so that I'm more aware than in my non-meditative state, I contemplate Principle #1, my Foundation. I become aware of all of the things affecting, or that I can affect with, my character, integrity, my health and the like. I take all of those things now drawn to me by this wide spectrum of knowledge and apply it to all of my successes, mistakes, education, "dummy taxes" paid, and the people and things in my life. Then I ponder how can I empower and give back to the universe, as well as what I want to manifest and want to receive; all with the objective of making a lot of money, helping a lot of people, and having a lot of fun.

With Principle #1, my Foundation, firmly in place, be it for the day, week, month, year, or lifetime, I next look to Principle #2, my Guideposts. The clarity of my values will bring the velocity that I need so long as I weigh all of the effects to ensure I have balance, and thus stability. From there, I focus on creating some sort of idea of what exactly I want to manifest and how to do it most accurately. Now I have the confidence to attract whatever it is I want to, and make it happen quickly.

At this point, my meditation turns to Principle #3, the Manifestation. I go through all of the exercises of perspective – remembering appreciation and adding value to everything and everyone that I will or have encountered – and use my free will to take all of my energy to connect and stay connected to source or goodness, and not waste energy on things like ego. I then proceed to broader thoughts, about my interactions with others where I will be aligning, taking action and preparing for adjustment. And if I stay connected to source or reconnect if need be, and if I've been successful with my AAA Strategy, then there are even broader implications as I envision us manifesting collectively and sharing a great vision where our inspiration and empowerment of others takes the belief to the "nth" Power. If I can do it for myself, I can do it to the "nth" Power.

Now, I turn to the first of the Molecular Principles, Principle #4 – Discipline. Knowledge, skill and desire will lead to the effective habits that are necessary to allow us to be and stay connected to source. Performance takes discipline and is connected to our morale, which is, basically, our emotions. If our energy in motion is doing the right things, our morale will be higher and the performance of a sixty-four hour production day can be achieved. In life, there is value to all of this – a Penn Value. If you give more than you receive, thus emptying your vessel, you'll receive more than you will give the next time … and so it goes as the universe is infinitely abundant. It is the essence of the Ben Franklin and the Reverse Ben Franklin Effects; so long as we're connected to each other and source, we are investments in each other.

With this discipline, Principle #5 – Strategy can help take it to an even higher level. Knowledge is power. We know our mental waves are the strongest things we have going, so use them wisely. Then take all of your knowledge and make a plan. With the plan and the understanding of how to use your mental waves, put the energy in motion and so long as you're communicating effectively or even over-communicated, you'll be attracting more accurately and rapidly exactly what you desire.

As for greater efficiency, that comes from Principle #6 – Understanding; which is how we stay connected to source, the final tool; as misunderstanding leads to corroded connections. We expand our comfort zone in the understanding of ourselves in order to transition into the learning zone, which is the most efficient place to be in order to stay connected to goodness. The Press is the method to apply the pressure to stay in the learning zone and stay connected. This enables us to shift the paradigm and expand our horizons as we now understand things in a different way, and have a different perspective than others. Finally, we can stay connected to goodness longer by maximizing the momentum or energy we've created.

Where this all takes us is up to each one of us, but, as I said, for me as well, it is still a learning process. Not too long ago, I lost $200,000 to a swindle, because I relied on mistakes made in due diligence done on my behalf. I had to tell my wife, but I was out of town when I found out about my loss. I felt conflicted about whether to call Julie and let her process what had happened or wait until I saw her in person. I decided to wait until I arrived back home, but, because of extenuating circumstances, I couldn't tell her right away. Once I told Julie, all of the negative energy – the blame, shame and justification about the person who had made the mistake in the due diligence (after all, the decision to proceed was ultimately all mine; I was the one accountable) as well as for me not having told Julie earlier (because it reminded me of how I had damaged my family eight years ago) – was gone. My wife's reaction of support, understanding and empathy was a both a huge relief and very much appreciated.

The swindle was ultimately a part of a much bigger legitimate transaction that I am in the midst of as I write this. And as crazy as it might sound, but for the swindle, the bigger deal would not be going forward! Ultimately, my hope is that I will have manifested what I wanted and, if not this go-round, there will have been a reason, and I'll continue to connect because I trust the universe and have no doubt that it'll happen when the time is right. In the interim, it will become a valuable part of my experience and my journey.

The last thing I mediate on is destination and what stage of empowerment I am at, not just as a whole, but also in a business situation. Yes, as the previous example demonstrates, the stages of empowerment – driving, striving, thriving, arriving, diving, reviving – are equally applicable on the microcosmic level – such as the status of a business deal and where it's going – as they are on the macrocosmic level – such as in regards to where I am in life. When we say something "takes on a life of its own", I take it to mean like life itself, that "something" has identifiable stages. That's why we need to strive, persevere and stay connected on a daily basis. If I feel that I was 90% successful on a given day, yes, I'll work on the other 10%, but I'll also take comfort in the fact that being 90% successful is better than being 89% successful. And, for all I know, I may only be at a 30% level in the grand scheme of the universe ... but I don't know any better. It's all perspective, and the fact that I know that I don't know is enlightenment to me. I'm still learning about how powerful this all is and how the universe works. Truth be told, if I find out that I'm only at a 30% success level right now, I'll get even more excited, given how powerful it has been so far, since I know I'm much better, faster and more accurate at connecting to source and goodness and empowering others to do the same. So I think to myself, "Imagine what will happen if I'm really successful 90% of the time!"

Regardless, I self-evaluate and constantly remind myself every day when I've done something or I haven't done something. This allows me to increase my learning zone as well as my comfort zone day by day. Sure, I make mistakes; but when I make mistakes, I correct them so they don't become cumulative. When I feel out of balance, I meditate to put myself back in balance. When I have successes, I try to scale and repeat them. And the things I value continue to thrive.

Okay, it's time for you to break from the huddle, and on count, shout an inspirational word to start the action on the playing field of life. You take your position: you're the quarterback who's connected to goodness. You've studied this playbook, you're ready for the snap of the ball, ready to thrive; even to call an audible if an adjustment needs to be made. You look left and right to your teammates – those people in your life who are closest to you – and you know that who you are being will empower them to be and do their best as well. You hear the cheers from the home crowd in the stands, and you realize that your performance on the field will, indeed, be collective; to the "nth" Power as the affect reaches a much broader audience – those who are not physically present and in your sphere of awareness – but who you will have an important, perhaps life-changing impact on nonetheless.

"Ready ... On Three. One, Two ... CONNECT!"

ACKNOWLEDGMENTS

I would like to thank the following people for assisting me on my journey:

First and foremost my wife Julie, Marissa, Mia, Marlena, Miles, my mom Karen, Aunt Marilyn, Uncle Eli, and the rest of my family, including Warren Moon (who is family to me), Scott Carter (also family), Leigh Steinberg, Harrison Lebowitz, Mike Sullivan, Cliff Carle, Colleen Maloy and the rest of my Angels, Rob Blake, Rage Richardson, my mentors including Dr. Wayne Dyer, Dr. Sangeeta Sahi, Lee Brower, Dean John Kramer, Professor A.N. Yiannopoulos, Vance Opperman, Lou Lombardi, Bill Gates, Ramon Desage, Michael Dell, Sean Parker, Jack Canfield, Dr. Michael Beckwith, Paul Allen, Leslie Buckley, Carl Fisher, Albert Einstein, Max Planck, Steve Jobs, and Walt Disney, all of the past and present employees and interns at Sports 1 Marketing, and all other people who I have come across directly or to the "nth" Power.

BIBLIOGRAPHY

BOOKS

Byrne, R. (2006). The Secret. Hillsboro, OR: Atria Books/ Beyond Words

Hill, N., Cornwell, R. (2004). Think and Grow Rich!: The Original Version, Restored and Revised. San Diego, CA: Aventine Press

Jordan, W.G. (2009), The Majesty of Calmness; individual problems and possibilities. Book Jungle (trade paperback)

Roosevelt, T. (1970). The Strenuous Life. Carlisle, MA. Applewood Books

Sun Tzu. (2009). The Art of War. El Paso, TX. Paso Norte Press

MAGAZINE

The Jim McMahon story in the Preface is excerpted from Rich Cohn's article, Da Bear, in Sports Illustrated, Oct. 28, 2013; from his book MONSTERS: The 1985 Chicago Bears and the Wild Heart of Football (Farrar, Straus, and Giroux; 2013)

ADDITIONAL BIOGRAPHIES

HARRISON LEBOWITZ

Harrison is an attorney and author. On the writing front, his works include, among others: the screenplay, *Le Boucher* (optioned by Rona Edwards Productions); the whimsical novel, *Go East, Young Man* (Sleeping Dog Press); the book, music, and lyrics for *Special Deliveries* (NYC and Vermont Actors' Repertory Theatre/Paramount Theatre productions); development of the TV procedural drama, *Serving Justice*, with Dawn Abel, Executive Vice President, CBS; development and host of a new program for the upstart New England Food and Travel Network; and contributing writer to the Emmy-Award winning PBS series, *Venturing*. He recently completed a new screenplay, *The Last Resistance Fighters*.

Harrison has two children, Tess and Jared, and lives in California.

MIKE SULLIVAN

Mike is The Official Artist of The Ronnie Lott IMPACT Trophy awarded annually and broadcast nationally on FOX to the best defensive player in college football each year. His original paintings as well as his limited editions are featured in many venues and private collections around the world. He has served as The Official Artist of The Best Damn Sports Show Period (Fox Sports Net) where his paintings of Chicago Bear RB Walter Payton and NBA legend Dr. J were featured on the permanent set. His original works have also been displayed on other TV broadcasts including shows on ABC, ESPN, Direct TV, HBO and FOX. He is currently creating a series of 25 original murals at major stadiums and venues that began with his first mural of Pat Tillman at ASU's Sun Devil Stadium in Tempe, AZ. Recent murals include one at DKR Memorial Stadium in Austin, TX (University of Texas), Jackie Robinson Stadium (UCLA Baseball) and The Los Angeles Memorial Coliseum (USC Football) in LA. His artwork has also raised money for many charities and foundations including The Magic Johnson Foundation, The Pat Tillman Foundation, Miller Children's Hospital, Kurt Warner FTF Foundation, Hannah and Friends and the Orangewood Pals/Hillview Acres charity.

Mike's work continues to grow as he focuses on the human figure in sports and play, as well as other subjects created in his unique "chiseled" style of painting.

For more information and updates go to:
www.davemeltzer.com
and:
www.sports1marketing.com